Handwritten note:

Hae Jo

I this [...] years now. And you [...] you have made out of your labor. Bill H. is my best friend. He is the replacement of the brother I lost 40 years ago. I think you will enjoy this book Life. Begin by reading the Introduction p. 10. God Bless you and your family.

Hugh Jam

4/5/19

SPIRITUAL COMMON SENSE

77 Guiding Principles for a More Meaningful Life

By

Bill Halamandaris

Acknowledgments

We are all indebted to others for the quality of our lives. Many of those to whom I am indebted are apparent in what follows, but I would particularly like to express my appreciation to my wife and soul mate, Angie Halamandaris; my mentor, Viktor Frankl; and my family at The Heart of America Foundation.

I am indebted to Hugh H. Jones, Jr. for many things, including a comment that focused this project and lead to its title. Together, we talked through many if not all of these principles. Mariele Jones deserves a special word of thanks for her editorial assistance. Sister Carol Rigali was kind enough to review an early copy of this manuscript and provided valuable guidance and assistance.

For Will

SPIRITUAL COMMON SENSE
77 Guiding Principles for a More Meaningful Life

Introduction

I.   The Meaning of Life

Introduction

My Son, as this is written, I do not know how long I will be around. The illness that struck me came out of nowhere. Until last fall, I had never been hospitalized, never had a broken bone, and never had a health concern greater than seasonal allergies and the common flu.

Suddenly, I found myself severely ill, with chills and fevers spiking well above 100, and white blood counts twice the normal range. My joints and the muscles in my legs ached so badly it was difficult to move.

Clearly, my body was fighting something, the doctor's said, but no one had any idea what. Despite the best efforts of some of the best physicians at George Washington University Hospital, Johns Hopkins and the Mayo Clinic, we still don't know. The exit conference at Mayo left me with the guidance that at some point whatever it was would declare itself. Then again, it might not. No one knows.

While I was hospitalized, my greatest fear was that I might not be there for you as you grow up. There is so much I want to tell you and so much you need to know.

Start with this: Despite what you now see and whatever concerns you may later have, I consider myself the most fortunate person I know. You and your mother are first among the many blessings in my life. When I look back as I did in writing this, I can't help but wonder how I got so lucky.

No one on earth could have charted the path I have taken. It brought me from a small mining town out west to Washington, D.C., which seemed at the time the center of the known universe. It gave the son of a coal miner with a 6th grade education an opportunity to go to college and law school, work with and learn from some of the best and brightest men and women of our time.

The lessons that follow reflect this journey. While the perspective on these principals is personal, I believe their truth is universal. They are part of our common sense, the term given to our shared understanding of what is fundamentally right and true. "In uncommon degree," Samuel Taylor Coleridge said, "common sense is what the world calls wisdom."

While I do not know what the future holds for me, in truth no one ever can. The future is promised to no man.

But of this, I am most certain: I will always be with you. Know now and then that I truly believe these principles will guide you to a life of meaning and purpose.

I. THE MEANING OF LIFE

MAN'S MISSION STATEMENT

*"He who loves best his fellow man is serving
God in the holiest way he can."*
...Confucius

Shortly before his death, Albert Einstein was
interviewed by the editor of a scientific
publication. The interview ranged across the
breadth of Einstein's work, including the
mysteries of quantum physics, his attempt to
read the mind of God, and develop a unifying
theory for the universe.

As they were wrapping up, the interviewer
said he had one final question.

"Why are we here?" he asked.

When Einstein did not immediately reply, the
interviewer became embarrassed and
apologized for asking something so difficult.

Einstein smiled gently.

"If I looked puzzled," he said, "it is because you asked me something so simple. We are here to serve one another."

Through the generations, from culture to culture, religion to religion, Moses to Mohammed, Buddha to Christ, whenever men ask the fundamental question of existence, the answer is the same. The Torah reminds us "deeds of love are worth as much as all the commandments of the law." Christians are bound to "love one another as I have loved you." Followers of Islam are taught that "whatever good you do for others, you send before your own soul and shall find with Allah, who sees all you do," while the religions of the East – Hinduism and Buddhism – express the same thought with their admonition to "hurt none by word or deed and be consistent in your well-doing."

From this fundamental truth, reflected in these differing ways of saying the same thing, flows man's mission statement. Everything we do that matters is done in response to this central law of life.

Everything that lasts is created out of love and concern of one human being for another.

Contrary to popular opinion, the secret to success in life has more to do with our hearts than our heads. What makes us different is not our ability to think but our ability to love.

GOD'S HANDS

"Whatever there is of God and goodness
in the universe, it must work itself
out and express itself through us.
We cannot stand aside
and let God do it."
...Albert Einstein

Albrecht Durer, generally regarded as the greatest artist of the German Renaissance, was one of 18 children born to a goldsmith in a tiny village near Nuremberg. As a boy, Durer worked at every job he could find to help put food on the table, while dreaming of becoming an artist.

Finally, his dreams began to come true when he was sent to work for a skilled artisan in Nuremberg. There he met and became friends with another man who shared the same dream. The two men moved in together, promising to support each other until they became established.

When this proved more difficult than they anticipated, Durer's friend offered to postpone his career and find work to provide food and shelter until Durer could generate enough income from the sale of his paintings and engravings to support them both. And so, while Durer continued refining his talents, his friend put aside his own aspirations and sought whatever work he could find.

Durer's friend scrubbed floors, washed dishes, and served in a nearby restaurant until the day came when Durer brought home enough money from the sale of a wood carving to support them both for some time. Only then did Durer's friend return to his art, but by this time his hands had lost their touch and his fingers could hardly hold a paintbrush.

Not long thereafter, Durer returned to the apartment the two men shared to find his friend kneeling in prayer, his hands folded reverently. Struck by the beauty of his friends hands, scarred and marked as they were by his labor of love, Durer was inspired

to create what many consider his masterpiece
– The Praying Hands – a tribute to his
friend's sacrifice.

In some way and in similar fashion, each of us has benefited from the sacrifices others have made on our behalf. Each of us is indebted to others. Each of us is called to respond. We are God's hands. Each of us holds the answer to someone's prayers.

THE MOST SELFISH THING
WE CAN DO

"No one has learned the meaning of life until
he has surrendered his ego to the
service of his fellow man."
...W. Beran Wolfe

Rachel Rossow has twenty-one children.
Though she would not acknowledge a
distinction between the children of her body
and the children of her heart, society would
say that nineteen of these children were
adopted.

All of the children Rachel chose to bring
home were born with severe mental or
physical handicaps. Some are mentally gifted
while physically challenged. Others are
physically gifted while being mentally
challenged. And some are seriously
challenged in all aspects of life.

When I came to know Rachel, I was surprised to learn that she considered her family to be like any other family, just a little larger than most. I couldn't help wondering how she met the enormous challenge presented by children with such diverse abilities. Trying to be as artful as possible, I asked her what she taught them. Rachel's response went directly to the heart of the question I meant to ask, but could not figure out how to phrase.

"I teach them all the same thing," she said. "First, you have to get to know yourself. Then you have to learn to love yourself. And then, you have to learn to forget yourself in service to others."

Knowing yourself, she explained, means understanding where you come from, who you really are, what gifts you were given, and what gifts you have to give. Loving yourself has nothing to do with narcissism and is the antithesis of ego. Loving yourself means embracing yourself as you truly are rather than as you wish to be. It comes from the understanding that everything is a gift.

Our weaknesses are as much a part of our uniqueness as our strengths.

But to be bestowed with meaning, life must transcend itself. To be fulfilled, we must learn to forget ourselves in service to others. In the words of George Sand, "There is only one virtue, the eternal sacrifice of self."

The most selfish thing we can do is be selfless. We have not started living until we can rise above the narrow confines of our personal interests to the broader concerns of society. It is by sacrificing ourselves that we sanctify our lives.

YOU GET WHAT YOU GIVE

"There never was a person who did anything
worth doing that did not receive
more than he gave."
...Henry Ward Beecher

Almost a hundred years ago, a Scottish farmer heard a cry from a swamp near his farm. When he ran to see what was happening, he found a boy stuck to his waist in the muck, struggling to set himself free. Without hesitation, the farmer extended a hand and rescued the boy from what otherwise would have been a slow and terrifying death.

The following day a fancy carriage pulled up to the Scotsman's humble cottage. A well–dressed man stepped out and introduced himself as the nobleman who owned a nearby estate. He said he was the father of the boy the farmer had rescued and that he had come to thank and repay the farmer.

The Nobleman held out a bag of coins but the farmer immediately replied, "I can't accept payment for what I did. It wouldn't be right. Besides, I have a son of my own."

At that moment as if he had been listening for his cue, the farmer's son came to the door.

"Is that your boy?" the nobleman asked and when the farmer nodded went on to say, "Let me repay you then in this fashion. You have helped my son. Let me help yours. Let me pay for your son's education. If he is anything like his father, he will make us all proud."

The farmer agreed and the farmer's son fulfilled the nobleman's prophecy. He excelled in school and went to St. Mary's Hospital in London to study medicine. He later earned international acclaim in the scientific community for his medical discoveries and was awarded the Nobel Prize for Medicine in 1945.

Ironically, at about the same time the son of the nobleman once more found his life in danger. This time, he was stricken with pneumonia. As he hovered on the brink of life, his physicians administered a new drug called penicillin and the boy, now a man known to the world as Winston Churchill, was again saved.

The benevolent nobleman was his father, Lord Randolph Churchill. The farmer's name was Fleming. His son was Sir Alexander Fleming, the discoverer of penicillin.

The patterns of the universe are not always so clear but they are always present. The universe is one piece. No good deed is ever wasted. Causes become effects. Effects become causes. What goes out from us comes back to us in equal kind, measure, and degree.

THE BOY WITH NO BRAIN

*"If any organism fails to fulfill its
potentialities, it becomes sick,
just as your legs would
wither if you never walked."*
... Rollo May

Benjamin Rossow, one of Rachel's kids, was
born without a brain. All he was given was
the cerebral cortex, a brain stem, to guide his
actions.

The potential quality of Ben's life and the
possibilities of his birth were judged so
limited, the learned men of medicine who
brought him into the world concluded there
was no point to his life. A boy without a
brain would never run with a football, grow
up to be a doctor or a lawyer, or contribute in
any meaningful way. He would never walk
or talk or have any hope of sustaining
himself.

Besides, they said, it was unlikely he would live more than year under the best of circumstances. They decided the best thing to do was to just let him go.

They never asked Ben, of course, and if they had he could not have answered. But fortunately, Rachel answered for him and took him home to be part of her remarkable family.

When I met Ben a dozen years later, I saw him respond in ways the establishment said would not be possible when he was born and still cannot explain. Benjamin tracked his mother with his eyes, responded to her embrace, and laughed when she laughed. He not only knew *who* she was, he knew *where* she was all the time.

Ben was a pure person. He knew nothing of prejudice, never learned to hate, and had never even dreamed of harming another person. All he knew was love - the love he was given and the love he gave - and that love enabled the child who it was said would never make a difference to change the Baby Doe laws in three states.

Most of us live with doubts that inhibit our actions. Our fears often create failure and an ever lengthening list of unrealized possibilities filed under what-might-have-been. Benjamin, on the other hand, never knew doubt and had no fear. As a result, while most of us only use a fraction of our potential, he was performing at least at 150 percent of what was said to be his capacity.

Simply stated, the basic principle of evolution is that what is used develops. Birds don't fly because they have wings; they have wings because they fly. It is not our impossibilities that fill us with despair, but rather the possibilities we have failed to actualize. The greatest defeat a man can suffer is the distance between what we are and what we can be.

THE INDISPENSIBLE INGREDIENT

"God is a verb."
   ...Buckminister Fuller

Some learned men from Stanford came to study Ben when he was nine. A boy without a brain could not have a memory. Without a memory, each and every experience would be new and learning would be impossible.

How then could Ben possibly recognize his mother? How could he laugh, react, and follow her? How could he have had such an impact on people around him? How was it possible for him to do any of the things it was said he could do?

They wired Ben up and watched. They played music, made faces, talked to him, and waited in vain for a response. For hours, the cameras recorded no discernible voluntary action. Ben's eyes were vacant and disinterested. Apparently, no one was home.

Then Rachel returned from work. The moment she walked in the door, Ben somehow knew she was there. Though she was three rooms away, he felt her presence. When she entered his bedroom, his eyes immediately found and followed her.

He smiled. He laughed. And when *she* played music he danced, his hands and feet moving in an awkward rhythm.

Stunned, the scientists sought a scientific answer and had to admit they were stumped. There was no way they could explain the things he did – perhaps because they did not know and perhaps because a scientist is loath to list love as a cause of action.

Yet, what is the one indispensable ingredient in life? What is the only way one person can positively influence another? What is the only thing we can never get enough of and the one thing we can never give enough? There is only one answer. The answer is love. It's love that acts.

CHILDREN OF THE NIGHT

*"The ultimate lesson all of us have to learn is
unconditional love, which includes
not only others but ourselves as
well...Love has no claims.
Love has no strings or expectations."*
... Elisabeth Kubler-Ross

The girl looked like nothing so much as what
she was - an awkward adolescent, with pale
hair and a plump body trying to make the
painful transition into adulthood - and
nothing so little as what she had been - a
prostitute working the streets of LA.

This was no *Pretty Woman* fantasy of happily
ever after for the hooker with a heart of gold.
This was the cold hard reality of a young girl
forced to live on the streets because the
streets were safer than her home, the
kindness of strangers more constant and
reliable than the concern of her kin.

In testimony to the depth of the scars left by her childhood, the first place she worked was the small town where she was raised and her father served as sheriff.

"Didn't it occur to you that he was bound to find out?" I said.

"Did it occur to you that maybe that is why I did it?" she responded.

The girl was one of a dozen I met at Children of the Night and one of thousands Lois Lee, the program's founder, has rescued from the streets. In the process, my perception of prostitution was forever changed. Until that time, I always looked down or looked away. Thanks to Lois, I came to understand the distance between *us* and *them* is not so far.

In our own way, many of us spend our whole life prostituting ourselves. We live with the illusion that we can buy love with good behavior, good grades, material things, success, or money. Often, we become what our parents want us to be, do what our children want us to do, behave the way our friends want us to behave in the hope that they will love us or love us more. At the same time, much of what we do not do, we do not do out of fear we will not be loved if we do.

We are responding to the subtle message of conditional love, which begins to be communicated at an early age. It comes disguised as "if". I will love you *if* you graduate from college, *if* you become a doctor, *if* you look the way I want you to look, *if* you marry well. I will love you even more *if* you give me what I want, *if* you do what I tell you to do, *if* you behave in a way I find acceptable.

The "ifs" populate the psychiatrists' offices, distort our self-image, and fill us with insecurity and doubt. In accumulation, the "ifs" can kill you. Many of the most prevalent diseases of our time result from our frantic search for acceptance and love.

But in our hearts, we know love can neither be bought nor sold. Love is a gift of a willing heart or it is nothing. Conditional love is a manifestation of the ego and a reflection of a desire to control. To be real, love must be unconditional.

SEEDS OF HOPE

"Give light and the darkness
will disappear of itself."
...Erasmus

During the darkest days of World War II,
England stood alone. "Everyone knew there
was no way we could survive," Jane Goodall
recalls, "with only a tiny strip of water
between us and the Nazis."

England did survive, of course, and the allies
ultimately prevailed. The reason, many
would say, was one man, Winston Churchill,
who believed they could. As one historian
observed, Churchill marshaled the English
language into combat against Nazi Germany
and people responded.

Though only a child at the time, Jane
remembers the power of Churchill's words.
"He said we would fight them in the air, we
would fight them on land and sea and we

would prevail. He said we would never give up and he was right. We won when no one thought we could possibly win."

More than half a century later, Jane is still influenced by Churchill's example. When she speaks to children, marshaling her words to fight the destruction of the environment, another war many say cannot be won, she almost always cites Churchill's example, saying the seeds of hope he planted took root in her soul, allowing her to extend the same hope and inspiration to many others.

"Every person matters," Jane says. "Everyone can make a difference."

It only takes a single ray of light to penetrate the dark. The world becomes better and brighter each time we are thoughtful and kind, each time we seek to help or heal, each time we care. The light dims each time we turn our backs in indifference and walk away.

WHERE IS GOD?

"We all sit around in a circle and
suppose, but the secret
sits in the center
and knows."
...Robert Frost

A man whispered, "God, speak to me."
A bluebird answered; but the man did not
hear.

The man called louder, "God, speak to me."
Thunder rumbled in the distance; but the man
did not notice.

"Let me see You," the man then said.
The sun rose and the sun set; but the man did
not see.

"Show me a miracle!" the man demanded.
At that moment a baby was born; but the man
was not aware.

"God, touch me," the man finally cried out in despair, "let me know You are here."

God reached down and touched the man. Annoyed, the man brushed the butterfly away and walked on.

God is everywhere. His gospel is written in the stars, in the trees and flowers, and every blade of grass. "Whatever is, is in God," Spinoza observed. "God is at the heart of everything."

THE LANGUAGE OF THE HEART

*"Meditation is a heart-to-heart
conversation with God."*
... St. Teresa

After living without heat and light for two
months and being unable to feed her
children, Bea Gaddy resorted to prayer.

"I asked the Supreme Being to show me how
to take care of my children," she said. "I did
not ask for anybody else's children. I just
wanted to know how to feed my children and
myself."

Bea had been homeless most of her life.
Hunger was her constant companion. As a
child, she went looking for food in her
neighbors' garbage cans. As an adult, she
had spent most of her life on welfare.

After years of trying to scrape by, Bea was
finally brought to her knees. In desperation,

her soul cried out for help. With her prayer, Bea sent a promise.

"Show me how to do this thing and I promise I will forever give back," she said. "I will walk with the people."

Bea's prayer was answered in a flash of inspiration that connected her present to her past. The next day, she asked her pastor if she could borrow a garbage can that had wheels.

While her neighbors in Patterson Park watched in disbelief, Bea wheeled it up to a grocery store on the corner and found the courage to ask the owner for the food that he was going to throw away that night. To her surprise and delight, the store owner filled the can with bread, fruit, vegetables and other perishable products.

Now that she knew what to do, Bea expanded the process. Soon she had so much food she was able to open an emergency center and feed hundreds of people each day. That fall out of gratitude, Bea initiated what became the largest annual Thanksgiving dinner in the country, feeding more than 25,000 people in Baltimore every year.

Prayer is not an intellectual process where we list our desires like a child writing Santa. Prayer is the language of the heart. It comes from the core of our being, the essence of ourselves. Whenever we are talking to ourselves in utmost sincerity and ultimate solitude, we are talking with God. In our deepest prayers, we pour out our hearts. God fills us up in response.

MAN'S HIGHEST ATTRIBUTE

"By compassion we make other's misery our
own and so by relieving them
we relieve ourselves also."
...Sir Thomas Browne

On April 23, 1975, a C5A evacuating 400 of
children from Vietnam to the United States
crashed shortly after takeoff. Half of the
children were killed immediately. Many
others were said to be maimed and injured.

The children on board were orphans under
the care of the Shoeshine Foundation, chaired
by Bob Macauley. When Bob heard what
had happened, he called the State Department
and asked them the status of their relief
efforts.

"Don't worry," he was told. "We will have a
plane there in 72 hours."

Macauley reminded the State Department that many of these children were infants. He knew they would not live long without assistance and said so.

Again, the response came, "We are doing the best we can."

For most of us that would have been the end of it; but for Macauley it would just be the beginning. Bob decided to charter a jet to rescue his kids.

"I called Pan Am and asked them what it would cost," Bob recalled. "They said a quarter of a million, ten percent down. I told them to put the plane in the air and I would put a check in the mail."

What Bob didn't tell them was that he didn't have $25,000 at that time.

"This all happened on a Friday," he explained. "By the time Pan Am got the check I knew it would be Monday. I figured the kids would be safe by then and we could worry about the rest later."

Sure enough, on Sunday morning Pan Am called to say the plane was on its way and that they wanted the balance. Bob wrote them another check, putting his house up for collateral until funds could be raised to relieve his debt of honor.

"When I see children in need," Bob said, "I see my own children. Once you have children of your own you can never look at a suffering child the same way again."

Compassion is man's highest attribute. Often, even our best instincts have a base side. Love, hope, faith, courage, and loyalty can all be corrupted by ego, selfishness, and human frailty. Compassion stands alone, unyielding, forging a bridge that connects our lives by a thousand sympathetic threads.

<u>30 SECONDS</u>

*"At the end of life, you never hear anyone
say, 'I wish I'd spent more
time at the office.'"*
...Barbara Bush

"Maybe what happened to me was what had
to happen to me to get my attention,"
Christopher Reeve said.

He was talking candidly with a small group
of people at a private reception in New York
after an event organized by my friend Tim
Love.

"I used to think nothing of taking a half
million dollars for filming a 30 second
commercial just to have money to fly my jet.
But what happened changed me," Chris
concluded.   "Now I know the world can
change in 30 seconds and I don't want to
waste a minute."

In economic terms value is defined by scarcity. The more commonly available a commodity is the less valuable it becomes regardless of its usefulness or necessity.

Thus, gold is more valuable than silver and silver more valuable than lead. Oil is more valuable than water and will be so until the not too distant future when water that is potable becomes so scarce its value escalates beyond all reason.

Great value is also attached to activities not commonly available, lifestyles above the norm, and the accumulation of things indicative of great wealth, power, or prestige. But while the market sets the value of things that are finite, the infinite is beyond measure.

For Chris the most precious thing in life became the time he had with his wife and family. He turned down tens of thousands of dollars just to see his son play hockey.

The only things of real value in life are the things that cannot be replaced. The palace can be rebuilt. A coliseum can be reconstructed. Every material thing can be

bought and sold but each moment is unique.
Every life is precious and irreplaceable.

THE MEASURE OF MEANING

"A candle loses nothing of its light
by lighting another candle."
...James Keller

My grandmother was a simple straightforward woman known for her faith and honesty. Like many of her generation, she came armed with a store of simple truths she visited upon us with whatever frequency circumstances required.

Many of her thoughts were familiar expressions on common themes, but the one that stays with me is an observation I have never heard before or since. It is a simple test for what is real and true, the measure of meaning and value in life.

"If you have something of value," she would say, "share it. If you can't share it isn't valuable."

On its face this observation is counterintuitive. But the more closely you look at it, the easier it is to discern the depth of this truth.

Grandmother's admonition comes in two layers. The first asks you to consider what has real value in life. Are these things tangible or intangible? The second suggests the test is sharing.

God gave us two hands, it is said, so that we can receive with one hand and give with the other. If we are solely concerned with holding on to what we have, we can neither give nor receive. The more one gives, the more one has to give.

The things of greatest value in life are the things we can share without diminishing by sharing. In fact, most of these things cannot be perfected until they are shared. Sharing increases happiness, faith, joy and hope, while diminishing doubt, sadness, and sorrow.

THE GIFT OF PRIVILEGE

"As the duty is precisely corresponded to the power, it follows that the richer, the wiser, the more powerful a man is, the greater is the obligation upon him to employ his gifts in lessening the sum of human misery."
... John Randolph

No one I know is more accomplished than Bob Pamplin, Jr. No one I know is more driven to make appropriate use of his talents.

Bob is a businessman, farmer, minister, philanthropist, and the author of thirteen books. He holds eight earned degrees, has received countless honors and honorary degrees, and has had incredible financial success. He made his first million while still in college and is now perennially listed as one of the wealthiest men in America by Forbes and Fortune magazines.

But to be real, Pamplin believes, "Our own success must contribute to the success of others."

We are all the custodians of our gifts, the trustees of our talents. We will not be judged by what we have been given but by the use we make of what we have been given to us. The focus of Bob's life revolves around a determined effort to live up to his God-given potential.

"God loaned me the ability to be successful," he says. "It is my duty to make good use of the capital He has provided."

While there is a role for each of us, more is expected from those who have more. There is a burden that corresponds precisely to privilege, a different standard for the rich and the poor, the powerful and the power-less. The more we are given, the more that is required of us. Our duty is to become useful, not according to our desires, but according to our powers.

THE ESSENCE OF THE SOUL

"Love is not one of the attributes of God,
but the sum of them all."
...James Gibbons

A few years ago, I attended a lecture by the Dalai Lama at Lisner Auditorium in Washington, DC. While he said a number of remarkable things, what I remember most is the power of his presence.

Lisner is part of George Washington University. It is a large, sprawling place with three levels and room for several thousand people. We were all chatting away, waiting for the lecture to begin. Somehow, all at once, with no fanfare or announcement, all conversation collapsed into a sudden silence. Each of us knew the Dalai Lama had stepped on the stage.

I had the same sense of awareness when I met Mother Teresa. The energy around her was so strong you felt her presence before you had reason to know she was present.

Michelangelo captured the transmission of this energy on the ceiling of the Sistine Chapel. When you see it, you can almost feel the life force flow from God to man.

That same spark of Divinity is in all of us. In some, it ebbs, waiting for the will to act. In others, like the Dalai Lama and Mother Teresa, it blazes and rages so brightly that the resulting glow lights the world.

Love is the essence of the soul. It is expressed in energy. When the soul is expressed through a man's intellect, it is genius; when it breaks through his will, it is character; when it flows through his heart, it is compassion.

THE WATERBED PRINCIPLE

*"All the questions have already been
answered; but since no one ever
listens, we must always be
prepared to begin again."*
...Anonymous

Mike Wallace came through the door in the
wall where the one-way mirror had been
installed.

"I'm Mike Wallace with *60 Minutes*," he said
to a nervous little man facing a desk
strategically placed before the mirror, "did I
just hear you offer this man a kickback?"

Wallace expected fear, denial, or panic.
Instead, the salesman barely broke stride. He
nodded his head and went on with his pitch
either unaware or unconcerned.

We were in Chicago with a team of
investigators working for the U. S. Senate,

looking into abuses of the Medicare and Medicaid programs, focusing on clinical laboratories. We found these companies were charging the government twice as much as they were charging their own patients for the same tests. The business was so profitable many companies were offering huge kickbacks to doctors. The abuse was so blatant we were stunned. We called *60 Minutes* and asked them if they wanted to see what we had found. When they agreed, we repeated our interviews with the cameras rolling.

Wallace's piece, called the "Clinic on Morris Avenue," ran the day before our hearing. The following day, the story of our investigation was on the front page of every major paper in the country.

As a result, as we had hoped and intended, so much attention was focused on the problem that reform legislation was enacted within two months. We had achieved our objective. We were ready to celebrate and move on to other things.

And we did - only to find ourselves returning to the same problem two years later. And again three years after that.

While I worked at the Senate, we had the same experience with attempts to fix Social Security, efforts to prevent elder abuse, prosecute phony doctors, control government contractors, and nearly every other problem we investigated. I called it "The Waterbed Principle." You push down here and it pops up there.

I have since learned this experience is not peculiar to Congress or legislation. There will always be wars to end, diseases to fight, criminals to catch, and lives to rebuild following disasters. Physicists call it the Second Law of Thermodynamics. The poet, W. B. Yeats, makes the point more gracefully. "Things fall apart," he wrote in the *Second Coming;* "the center will not hold."

The battle of humanity must be fought day after day. There are no final answers or permanent solutions. We must always be prepared to begin again.

WHAT'S REAL?

"We are not human beings having a spiritual experience. We are spiritual beings having a human experience."
...Pierre Teilhard De Chardin

Everything material emerged from the immaterial. Every building is constructed on a design. Every design is based on an idea.

As Emerson observed, "thoughts rule the world." A thought precedes every action, change, or motion.

In this world, things only have the value we give them. There is no intrinsic value to the jewelry we wear, the cars we drive, the things we buy, or the coin and currency we use to make these transactions. The value of these things is supported by faith and a belief system that provides a symbolic value where there inherently is none. In different cultures, the same value is assigned to different symbolic currency.

The words we use to describe things are as inexact and conceptual as the things they describe. In other words, the words we use to describe things are not the things they represent. Words merely stand imperfectly for the things they represent in our minds.

Much of the confusion of our day-to-day conversations is a result of this process. The word "table" conjures up a flat surface supported by legs, but the image that comes to mind – the shape of the surface, the contour, height and even number of legs – is determined by our expectation and experience. Yet, when we say the word 'table' we all assume we are seeing the same thing.

We have it reversed. The material is immaterial. What is real is not what we can see but what we sense. Buildings crumble. Success fades. Flesh decays. We are not immortal, but our thoughts are.

II. HOW THE WORLD WORKS

FORGIVE AND FORGET

*"Let go. Why cling to the pain and the
wrongs of yesterday? Why hold on to
the very things that keep you
from hope and love."*
...Buddha

My Father had the best memory I have ever
seen. Unfortunately, much of what he chose
to remember had to do with the painful
episodes in his life.

Dad remembered every slight, every hurt,
every unkind word. Increasingly, as he grew
older, the story of his life became a chronicle
of pain as he resurrected his injuries and
regrets on a recurring basis.

Like my Father, many of us carry the scars of
old grievances and ancient hurts. The scars
remind us. We can forgive but not forget.

But saying, "I can forgive, but not forget," is just another way of saying, "I cannot forgive." Forgiveness, to be real, cannot be partial or half-hearted. "Forgiveness," Henry Ward Beecher wrote, "ought to be like a canceled note – torn in two and burned up, so that it never can be shown against us."

True forgiveness is not based on a sense of judgment, the belief the offending party has learned their lesson, or "paid for" their crime. True forgiveness is based on the understanding that such judgments are inappropriate and as wrong as the wrong we condemn.

Once we have forgiven, we must forget. The remembrance of forgiveness is like pulling a scab off an old wound. It re–infects what was trying to heal and trades a new wound for an old one. The injury we do to ourselves by holding on to our hurts is often far greater than the injury done to us by others.

Those who cannot forgive and forget can never heal. True forgiveness heals and makes all things new. It is as if the injury had never been.

THE MOST PERSISTENT QUESTION IN LIFE

"If I do not do this, who will do it?
If I do not do it now, when will I do it?
But, if I do it only for myself, what am I?"
...Hillel

When I met Peter Grace he had been a CEO longer than any man in corporate history. The grandson of the founder of W. R. Grace, Peter had taken the helm of the billion dollar company while still in his thirties. Now nearly ninety, he carried the scars of some fifty years on the public stage.

Grace had been lionized and vilified, praised for his visionary leadership and denounced for his aggressive business tactics. Respected, loved, and feared by his peers, few in corporate America had as much power.

To all appearances, Peter's life was an open book. Yet, the more I learned about him the more I found that like an iceberg the best part of him was concealed from public view. The list of his good works was endless.

When I asked him to tell me the greatest lesson in his life, Peter said that as a boy he was tutored by Father James Keller, founder of The Christophers.

"Whenever I came to him to describe some great horror I had heard about or some injustice in the world, Father Keller's response was always the same," Peter said. "As I finished describing whatever caused my concern, he would say -- 'Well, what are you going to do about it?"

This is the most persistent question in life. The crying of a child, the man on the street, the neighbor in distress all pose questions to which we must respond.

Every moment provides a chance. Every situation presents a challenge. Every problem is an opportunity. Life questions man. We must answer.

FAITH TRANSCENDS REASON

*"Without faith, nothing is possible.
With it, nothing is impossible."*
...Mary McLeod Bethune

There was no reason to believe Coe would be anything but trouble. Coe was the leader of the Bloods in Houston, a six foot seven, mountain of man with a reputation for violence.

Branded a threat to the community and feared even by the members of the gang he led, it was widely believed it would only be a matter of time before Coe was locked up or dead, a victim of violence or drugs or both. Then he met Grandma Edie.

Grandma Edie saw something of value buried beneath his tough exterior. She saw a boy who had been abandoned by his own family, told he was worthless, discounted by society, and never really given a chance. She saw the man he could be.

Grandma Edie took him in when no one else would have him. The authorities laughed, saying it was only a matter of time before he would find a permanent home – in the penitentiary or underground.

But faith transcends reason. For nearly a year, she held on when reason said it was time to let go. She battled his past, pulling him back in off the streets. She flushed pounds of drugs down the toilet, sobered him up and held him when he was sick. For nearly a year, she told him he had a future. Finally, he began to believe her.

When I met Coe three years later, he was calling Grandma Edie "Momma" and crediting her with giving him a new birth. He went on to attend a theological seminary in Texas with the intent of becoming a priest. Coe is so gentle and so soft-spoken it is hard to believe he once had blood on his hands.

No one could have predicted the road Coe has taken or where he will go. Nor can we be certain where our own path leads or where it will end. But even though we walk in doubt and darkness, faith tells us that we will find our way.

Nothing of value can be accomplished without faith. Without hope, we could not begin. Without faith, we could not finish.

BUILD THE CASTLE

"A rock pile ceases to be a rock pile the moment a single man contemplates it bearing within him the image of a cathedral."
...Antoine de Saint-Exupery

When they began building Disneyworld, the management team was immediately caught up in a raging debate. The question was how to proceed and in which order to tackle the buildings that formed this enormous construction challenge.

The technicians said the only way the project made sense was to proceed systematically, working from one end to the other, building roads and infrastructure as they went. The dreamers, led by Disney, wanted to start in the middle.

Disney wanted to build the castle first. Others argued it was the least practical structure in the project and the most difficult to construct. They said it should be held for future construction, the icing on the cake.

Disney responded the castle was the most important structure in the project and the only way to make the dream come alive. He wanted the construction crews to see where they were going and know what they were working toward.

In much the same way, a candle is kept burning in many churches as a sign of God's presence. For essentially the same reason, the gods of Greek mythology placed hope at the bottom of Pandora's box of troubles.

Hope sees the part of the glass that's half full and the opportunities presented by our problems. Hope opens doors despair closes and keeps us going when it would easy to quit.

Man cannot live without hope. After all is done that can be done, hope is what remains.

SEEDS OF THOUGHT

*"We find similar truths in the greater
literature of the world. The more
deeply authors penetrate into the
depths of human experience
the more they speak the
language of all humanity."*
...Rollo May

By most accounts, the thing we call "radio"
was born in 1895 when Guillermo Marconi
sent an electrical signal through the air from
one end of his house to the other. Most
people have never heard of Ferdinand Braun,
whose contribution was equally essential.

Marconi, the son of a wealthy Italian father
and an Irish mother, was schooled privately
and self-taught. He was quick to seize the
moment when he read an article suggesting
the possibility of using radio waves to
communicate. Once he was able to prove the

possibility, Marconi was equally quick to apply for a patent.

Marconi sent a radio signal across the English Channel in 1899 and across the Atlantic Ocean two years later. But before Braun's contribution, the furthest Marconi had been able to communicate was 50 kilometers.

Braun was a university professor with a doctorate from the University of Berlin. This man of science, who among other things later developed the picture tube found in most televisions before the digital age, never bothered to patent his discoveries. Instead, he published detailed descriptions of his experiments so that other scientists could duplicate his work.

Braun and Marconi shared the Nobel Prize for Physics in 1909 for their complimentary contributions to the development of wireless telegraphy. They join 110 others who have been simultaneously recognized for their work in physics. In fact, the Nobel Prize for Physics has been shared nearly half of the years it has been given.

Similarly, the Nobel Prize for Medicine has been shared more than half of the years it has been given. Some of these people were recognized for a team effort, but many were recognized for arriving at the same stunning conclusion independently at about the same time. The same pattern is apparent in politics, religion and every other sphere of human endeavor.

God rarely gives a truly big idea to only one person. The seed is simultaneously planted in many minds. The more critical the task, the more noble the goal, the more fundamental the truth, the more it is made part of our common consciousness.

SOUL MATES

"The children of the world are all separated
one from another because their
hearts are in different places; but the
children of God, having their heart where
their treasure is, and having only one
treasure which is the same God,
are consequently, always joined
and united together."
...St. Francis of Sales

It was a hot, sticky, summer day when Fred
Matser arrived at Baltimore International
Airport. He was on way to from Holland to
Los Angeles and had a brief layover. Dr.
Jerry Jampolsky, a mutual friend, said we
had so much in common and we had to meet.

I waited for Fred with only the vaguest of
descriptions. He could have been any of a
dozen people I saw coming out of customs.
But with no description of me at all, Fred

walked through the door and came toward me as I moved toward him.

Though there were dozens of people around who could as easily have matched his description, I knew him instantly and he knew me. As we talked, we found ourselves connecting on so many levels it was unsettling. It was as if we were long lost brothers who had suddenly found and recognized each other. We adopted each other on the spot to formalize our feelings.

Fred spends most of his time in the Netherlands, some six thousand miles and six time zones away; but ever since we met all I have to do is think of him and he will call. The first time this happened, I was startled. My wife and I were talking about Fred on the way home from church. I was wondering how he was and thought I would give him a call that afternoon. Within half an hour, Fred called for no apparent reason. He said he had been thinking of me.

The same thing has happened often enough through the years that I have come to take it for granted. It is like we are connected no matter how far we are apart. The more I have come to depend on my ability to connect on this level, the more I have found it with other people.

All humanity is indivisible, but some connections are always stronger. These are our soul mates. They break through the superficial barriers we erect to protect ourselves and remind us - there is no distance between souls.

TREAD LIGHTLY

"This we know. The earth does not belong to
man; man belongs to the earth...
Whatever befalls the earth befalls the
sons of the earth. Man did not weave
the web of life; he is merely a strand
in it. Whatever he does to the web,
he does to himself."
...Chief Seattle

Some forty years ago, Jane Goodall ventured
alone into the wilds of Africa to study
animals' relationship to man. Now her
primary concern is man's relationship to
animals and the respectful use of the planet
we share.

For generations, much of western civilization
was driven by the belief that we are
fundamentally different from the animals.
Mankind was placed on one side of the line
and all creation on the other. Now, thanks
largely to Jane, we have a better

understanding of the nature of things and how much we have damaged the web of life. Such is the depth of her concern, Jane left the forest she loves and now spends 300 days a year on the road, speaking about the destruction of the environment, and asking people to tread lightly on the earth.

It is said cancer occurs when one cell will not cooperate with the other cells adjacent to it. These errant cells with no concern for their host and no relationship with each other consume everything around them, destroying themselves in the process. With this perspective, it is tempting to wonder if the rest of creation might look at mankind the same way we look at malignant growths in our bodies.

According to the United Nations, half of the world's wetlands were lost in the 20th century, half the world's forests chopped down, and 70% of the world's major marine fisheries were depleted. In the next 30 years, we could lose 20% of all the species on earth. More than 30,000 species of plant life and 4,600 mammal species – one fourth of all mammals – are endangered.

To say we love God and exercise cruelty or show indifference toward other living things is a contradiction in terms. Life is sacred. It is the supreme value to which all other values are subordinate.

THE VOICE OF GOD

"God's love speaks to us in our hearts and
tries to work through us in the world.
We must listen to it as to a pure
and distant melody that
comes to us across the noise
of the world's doing."
..Albert Schweitzer

Benjamin Rossow, the boy without a brain, is credited with changing the Baby Doe laws in three states. When I asked his mother, Rachel, how this was possible she said it was a combination of the inspiration his example provided and the power of his presence.

"On several key occasions when the Connecticut Assembly was debating the first measure," Rachel said, "I got a call from a committee staff member saying the committee was deadlocked. She asked if I could come down and bring Ben. They didn't want me to testify. They just wanted

Ben to be there. We didn't say a word. We just sat quietly in a corner of the room while the Committee discussed their differences. That's all it took."

In my early years, my understanding of the voice of God was shaped by the movie "The Ten Commandments." Though I was just a boy, I still remember hearing God speak to Charlton Heston. Like everyone else, I sat transfixed in awe and wonder as a big booming voice laid down the fundamental laws of the Old Testament.

Dramatic as this is, Ben's story is probably closer to the truth. God speaks with silence. His alphabet is intuitive and instinctual.

God's voice is not limited, like a radio tower with a defined range, speaking solely certain souls with the capacity to tune in. It is omnipresent and compelling and there are more questions than commandments.

God is in the distance from what is to what ought to be. It is His voice that tells us right from wrong, offers the judgment that "someone should do something about that," and prompts our actions. What is disclosed to consciousness is something that is. What is revealed to the conscience is something that should be.

THERE IS ONE TRUTH

*"Though we may know Him by a
thousand names, He is one
and the same to us all."*
...Ghandi

The search for meaning and purpose, some
sense of religion or spirituality however it is
expressed, is part of the common heritage of
man. Nearly two thousand years ago,
Plutarch observed, "If you were to travel the
world over, you could find cities without
walls, without wealth, without coins, without
schools, or theaters, but we have yet to
discover a city without a temple or a society
that does not pray and worship."

Yet, and perhaps because man's relationship
with God is such a fundamental part of our
existence, no one has succeeded in capturing
the essence of this profound matter in a way
that is completely acceptable to all other
seeking souls. Rather, it seems our

81

experience is more akin to the parable of the nine blind men and the elephant – each describing in detail and with great conviction the small part of the whole they have sensed and discovered, while denying the perceptions of others, seeing a contradiction where there is none.

What unites us is far greater than what divides us. In the words of the Dalai Lama, "Every major religion of the world has similar ideals of love, the same goal of benefiting humanity through spiritual practice, and the same effect of making their followers into better human beings."

The accuracy of the Dalai Lama's observation is ratified on a daily basis by personal experience. We all have reason to know that holiness, compassion, selflessness, and charity are not the exclusive domain of any one faith. Every religion, every church, and every belief system has provided men and women of exemplary character.

God has no religion. In the world after and before this world, there is neither black, or white, male or female. There is no Hindu or

Buddhist, Jew or Gentle, Muslim or Christian, Protestant or Catholic. God is seated in the heart of all.

FREUD AND FRANKL

"We cannot render benefits to those from whom we receive them, or only seldom. But the benefits we receive must be rendered again line for line, deed for deed, to somebody."
... Ralph Waldo Emerson

Viktor Frankl was the founder of Logotherapy, the Third Viennese School of Psychotherapy, and the author of 32 books, including *Man's Search for Meaning*.

After reading *Man's Search for Meaning*, I sent Dr. Frankl a letter expressing my admiration. I told him I had stumbled on his book after an extensive period of soul-searching and that I wished I had found it earlier.

This book had a profound impact on me and I told him so. To my surprise, Dr. Frankl answered my letter with a personal note raising questions that encouraged a response. We exchanged letters several times after that before I found an opportunity to invite him to come to America to keynote a conference I was helping organize.

I met Viktor at the airport late one afternoon in 1986 and peppered him with questions as we drove to town. I continued my questioning over dinner and then reluctantly said goodnight.

The next morning, Viktor gave a stirring and thought provoking speech, receiving a standing ovation from the three thousand people attending the conference. As I went to the dais to escort him to a reception in his honor, he scribbled something on his notes and then handed them to me. When I looked at what he had given me, I found he had autographed the text of his speech and inscribed it with a personal note.

After lunch, I walked him back to his room and thanked him for making the long journey from Vienna for one speech. I said good-bye not knowing when, if ever, I would see him again.

Early the next morning, the phone rang at my home. When I answered, I heard Viktor's voice. He said his return flight did not leave until late in the day and he was wondering if I would mind coming down and spending some time with him.

We spent the entire day together. Though nothing explicit was said, I could tell he was "working on me." Viktor had clearly thought about the questions I had asked the day he arrived and was trying to extend my thinking. He probed and pushed with the gentle, thoughtful persistence of the good psychiatrist he was.

Afterwards, Viktor periodically sent me the text of something he was working on – a speech or an article – and asked what I thought. The question was always phrased as though he was seeking my opinion, but I came to know it was just one more way of extending our dialogue.

In much the same manner, I came to expect a periodic phone call. The ones I liked best were the ones where he said he was going to be somewhere in the United States and wondering if I could I find time to join him.

One of the last things Viktor sent me to review contained a portion of a chapter he was preparing for his autobiography. There was little Viktor left to chance and I expect there was no chance in this.

The text described his relationship with Freud. As a young man following the same path, Frankl said he was so eager to meet Freud that he staked out a park in Vienna that Freud was said to frequent, hoping to see him.

Finally, Frankl's effort was blessed with success and he was bold enough to make an approach. He described Freud as gracious, patient, and generous. At the conclusion of their conversation Freud was kind enough to invite Frankl to send him some of his work to review.

"Before long," Viktor wrote, "I was corresponding with Freud on a regular basis, sending him anything I thought would interest him. He promptly answered every letter and was responsible for publishing my first treatise on psychotherapy."

We are rarely ever to repay those who have helped us measure for measure. The only alternative is to pass it on. When we are engaged in helping others, we are not so much conferring favors as canceling debts.

THE CHAIN OF LOVE

*"Every man has a mission from God
to help his fellow beings."*
...James Gibbons

Truett Cathy's first business was selling
Coca-Cola door to door at the age of eight.
He is enough of a businessman to still
remember that he made a nickel profit on
each half dozen Cokes he sold. Later, he said
he began buying Cokes by the case – 24 for
80 cents – and thought "that was big
business."

After World War II, Truett started a
restaurant with his brother. It was so tiny it
was called the Dwarf House. The brothers
put $4,000 of their own money in the
restaurant and borrowed $6,000 more. "We
couldn't afford to fail," Truett says,
"because that was everything we had."

Today, that tiny restaurant has evolved into the chain of restaurants known as Chick-fil-A. Chick-fil-A is a multi-billion dollar company with thousands of franchise outlets in 39 states and an unparalleled record of 40 consecutive years of sales increases.

The key to this success, Truett says, was discovered 30 years ago at a corporate retreat. The purpose of the retreat was to reexamine Chick-fil-A's corporate structure and develop a mission statement that would govern all of the corporation's present and future activities.

After some deliberation, Cathy's team came up with the statement that still stands and guides their operations: To glorify God by being a faithful steward of all that is entrusted to us and to have a positive influence on all whom come in contact with Chick-fil-A.

That's a remarkable statement for any company, but particularly for one involved in the fast-food business. True to their purpose, Truett and Chick-fil-A have awarded millions in scholarships to restaurant employees, invested millions more in character-building programs for their customers' children, and established 11 foster care homes for disadvantaged children.

"The world was created for the purpose of giving," Truett explains. "Even the birds and the trees."

Life is a chain of love, which binds all things together. Everything provides something essential to something else. Plants and animals trade atoms and air. The water that falls on the earth passes through and is collected in the rivers, lakes, and oceans only to rise and fall again.

JOIN HANDS

*"Every person must feel responsibility to
discover his mission in life.
God has given each normal person
a capacity to achieve some end."*
...Martin Luther King

A few years ago, a three-year-old girl
wandered away from her home in Iowa into
the fields where she thought her parents were
working. When her parents returned, they
called for her and only became concerned
when she did not respond.

After searching their home to no avail, the
parents called their neighbors and asked for
help. The neighbors scattered across the
farm and searched without success for two
days. Finally, the leader of the search party
suggested they join hands, stretch out, and
march across the fields together. They did as
he suggested and finally found the little girl –
unfortunately, too late.

When she heard the news, the girl's mother dissolved in tears. "Why didn't we join hands before?" she cried.

The same question could be asked of our response to most of the persistent problems of the world. Is there any problem we could not solve if we all joined hands and worked together? Individually, we may only have a small piece of the puzzle but each of us has at least one piece and each piece is essential.

Community comes when people see hope where there is fear and decide to join hands, linking themselves with others in a common cause. Community comes when people decide not to ignore a problem or run away, but to reinforce each other and take on apathy and despair. Community comes when we realize nothing of real value can be accomplished alone.

THE GREATEST GOOD

*"We do not believe in ourselves until
someone reveals that deep inside
us something is valuable, worth
listening to, worthy of our trust,
sacred to our touch. Once we
believe in ourselves we can risk
curiosity, wonder, spontaneous
delight or any experience that
reveals the human spirit."*
... e. e. cummings

On the South side of Chicago, I met a young
man named Altheos. Not long before, he had
been pegged as a troublemaker. Ill-groomed,
sullen, defiant, and prone to violence, he was
thought to be incorrigible. The school was
ready to dismiss him until Corla Hawkins,
the teacher the kids call "Momma Hawk"
stepped in.

Momma Hawk asked that Altheos be given
one last chance in her classroom. She took

him in, mothered him, bathed him and fed him. She found out he lived with his grandparents in a run-down shack without running water and often without heat or electricity.

As she gained his trust, Altheos opened up. She found out the reason he got into so many fights was because the other kids made fun of his dirty clothes and the way he smelled. She told him that would now end, bought him new clothes and gave him the run of her house.

Rather than a troublemaker, she told him he was gifted. Together, she said, they would find out what his gift was. To everyone's surprise, it turned out to be hockey. Not long after I met Altheos, he graduated from the school that was ready to dismiss him and left for college on a hockey scholarship.

Ask anyone who has made a mark in the world how they got where they are and you will find they can readily identify one or two people who made a significant difference in their lives. Almost invariably, this person is someone like Momma Hawk who had an irrational belief in their future, someone who thought they would succeed in the absence of any direct evidence to support that conclusion.

The greatest good we can do is not to share our wealth with others but to reveal their own. When we treat other people as if they were what they ought to be, we help them become what they are capable of being. When we look for the best in others, we bring out the best in ourselves.

THE GOOD SAMARITAN

"All the sages, from Lao Tzu to Buddha to
Confucius to Jesus, have told
us that to experience the love
of God we must give our
love to those around us."
...Andrew Harvey

Kurt Weishaupt saw the handwriting on the wall. The Nazi's had invaded his homeland. He knew it was only a matter of time before they came for him.

He talked with his wife and they agreed they would make their way to Marseilles and from there to the Pyrenees where they could cross over into Spain. They left for Madrid with nothing but a train ticket to their name. Their money had been converted to British pounds, a currency declared invalid by the British because of German counterfeiting. With forged documents and without a penny to their name Kurt knew they were exposed and vulnerable.

As Kurt feared, the conductor checking tickets on the train looked at the Czech passport he had picked up in Marseilles and immediately recognized it as a forgery. Worse, the ticket agent was accompanied by a Gestapo officer.

Sixty years later, Kurt still trembled when he recalled the terror of hearing the agent call out – "This is a false document!"

At that moment, a door to a first-class compartment near them opened. Kurt heard someone he couldn't see say, "Don't molest these people. They are my friends."

The conductor stopped short, bowed and withdrew, taking the Gestapo with him. Kurt watched in disbelief, not quite certain what had happened. He was even more surprised when their benefactor stood up and called them into his compartment. He invited them to join him and told them everything would be all right.

"He took us to Madrid," Kurt said. "He brought us to a hotel, paid the bill in advance, and bought us some food. The next day, he picked us up in the afternoon, showed us the city, and then took us to dinner."

The following morning the Good Samaritan returned. He escorted the Weishaupts to the train station. He told them he had arranged for their travel and purchased tickets to get them safely out of Spain. He gave them some documents in Spanish, which he said should be presented to the border patrol, and three thousand pesetas for the journey.

"When we came to the Portuguese border," Kurt remembers, "we were again asked to present our passports. Everyone else on the train had to get out. But we were allowed to continue."

Kurt amassed a fortune in the United States. He never learned his benefactor's name. Nor does he know what moved this man to risk his life for a stranger. While it would be nice to know, he says it really doesn't matter. He is content to pass it on.

The life the Spaniard saved has blossomed to save hundreds of critically ill children. The man the Spaniard clothed and fed, has clothed and fed thousands in equal need and, like his benefactor, most of what he does he does anonymously.

No gift is truly ours until God has blessed someone else with it through us. What is given to us we are obligated to pass on to others.

THE PATH OF GOD

*"Every person, all events of your life are
there because you have drawn
them there. What you chose to do
with them is up to you."*
...Richard D. Bach

Janine found out she was HIV positive when
she was pregnant. She had known her
husband had engaged in the use of
recreational drugs before their marriage, but
he had assured her he was never addicted and
never used anything heavier that pot.

The knowledge that he had been an
intravenous drug user, coupled with the fact
that he had acquired the virus and passed in
on to his wife and still unborn child shattered
whatever trust remained in their relationship.
Shortly after their daughter was born, Janine
filed for divorce.

My wife met Janine when she brought her daughter to Give Kids the World. She fell in love with them both. Three years later when Angie and I were married, we asked them to be part of our wedding party. By this time, Janine had been diagnosed with cancer. While the HIV was seemingly under control, the cancer was raging. She wore a turban to camouflage the loss of hair caused by chemotherapy, looked pale and gaunt. She seemed content to watch the party from the sidelines until Ron Kolanowski, one of our groomsmen, unexpectedly asked her to dance.

As soon as they hit the dance floor Janine lit up. Everyone felt a sudden burst of energy. Within moments all other movement stopped as we watched these two move magically across the floor with a grace most of us can only imagine.

"No one has asked me to dance in years," Janine said later, still beaming with joy.

How did Ron know she wanted to dance when to all appearances she was incapable of it? There was no way for him to know she had been a dancer all her life or that she had taught dance and once aspired to a career as a professional dancer. Nor was there any way for him to know that she would pass away a few months later, wiggling and jiggling her arms and legs, sending the tubes attached to her body flying in a makeshift dance designed to cheer up those gathered around her deathbed. Was it a coincidence that brought the two best dancers in our party together for one last dance?

"Something called me to her," Ron later said. He felt compelled to ask her to dance and did so without even thinking.

There are no coincidences or casual occurrences. We may not know where the road we are on will lead, but we cannot stray far from the path God has designed for us. Every person in our lives is there for a purpose.

THE ROSETO PRINCIPLE

"Dostoyevsky said, 'If there is no God, then anything is possible.' I would say that if there is no love, nothing is possible. Man absolutely cannot live by himself."
... Erich Fromm

Fifty years ago, researchers began studying the importance of social connections in a small town in eastern Pennsylvania called Roseto. Roseto, whose settlers all came from the same village in southern Italy, suffered less than half as many heart attacks as the residents of the two nearest towns.

The three communities were found to be nearly identical in every respect except one. The lives of Roseto's residents were tightly woven together in a series of reinforcing social relationships involving nearly every aspect of the community.

When the second generation in the study began seeking independence and gave up the traditional ways, the heart attack rate in Roseto began to rise. By the third generation, the social dynamics of Roseto nearly matched those of the other two communities - as did the heart attack rate.

Other studies confirm the findings in Roseto. Loners are two to five times more likely to get sick and die prematurely than those with a social network. They are also less likely to recover from traumatic illness. In one study, researchers at Dartmouth found that patients without a social support system were four times more likely to die within 6 months of open heart surgery. The evidence of our interdependence is so strong, it is said, that if you smoke and don't belong to any social groups it is a statistical tossup whether you should stop smoking or join a club.

"As a rough rule of thumb," Robert Putnam writes in *Bowling Alone*, "if you belong to no groups and you decide to join one, you cut your risk of dying over the next year in half."

No individual stands alone, complete,
distinct, and unadorned. We need each other
to complete ourselves. Others act upon us as
we act on upon them. We shape the direction
of each other's lives much as wind affects the
tree's design. You can see even the slightest
breeze captured in the movement of the
leaves, but it is only with the passage of time
that we see how the tree has been inclined.

THE RESCUING HUG

"We are each of us angels with only one wing; and can only fly while embracing each other."
...Luciano de Crescenzo

A friend sent me an article called the "Rescuing Hug." It was one of those emails that make the rounds, the story of twin girls born prematurely. According to this article, the girls were so tiny they both had to be placed in incubators so that their conditions could be monitored.

The first born stabilized quickly. The other wasn't so fortunate. The doctors told the parents their second child might not live.

That was before a nurse thought to place the two babies together in one incubator. Almost immediately, the older of the two threw an arm over her sister in an endearing embrace. Within moments, the smaller baby's heart rate stabilized and her temperature rose to normal. A few weeks later, both were released and taken home in perfect health.

In much the same manner, our lives are intertwined and wrapped around each other. The contribution others have made to our lives is reflected in all we think and do. So tightly knitted are our lives that there would be little left of any of us if we were to discard what we owe to others.

It is for this reason that the world rarely makes sense from a personal point of view. There is no adequate explanation in personal terms for the differences between us. Why do some have so much and others so little? Why must some struggle when others have lives of such ease? Why are some so blessed and others so challenged?

The world only makes sense with detachment and distance. From a distance, we can see how the pieces fit. With detachment, we see that what happens to one more often than not is for the benefit of another.

THE TIE THAT BINDS

"There can be no unity, no delight of love, no harmony, no good in being where there is but one. Two at least are needed for oneness."
...George MacDonald

Uncle Nick married early. He and my aunt, Julia, were thirteen and fifteen when they met and seventeen and nineteen when they married. They lived together for more than 60 years, their lives revolving around each other. They were never apart.

Then, in their seventies, both Uncle Nick and Aunt Julia developed cancer. Aunt Julia was diagnosed with breast cancer. A few months later, almost as if he were keeping pace, Uncle Nick was diagnosed with colon cancer.

Aunt Julia passed away eighteen months later. Uncle Nick was devastated by her loss, but a stubborn man and a proud veteran of World War II, he battled on.

Finally, he had the satisfaction of hearing the doctors say he had won, but it was a hollow victory. Devastating and difficult as it was, the fight had given him something to live for. Now that they said he had won, he began to wonder what he had won.

Uncle Nick moved in with a friend and tried to get on with his life, but his heart wasn't in it. The cancer came raging back and this time it went quickly. It wasn't long before they said his days were numbered and that he could go at any time.

This time, Uncle Nick seemed at peace with his prognosis. He told everyone he was ready to go. He said he looked forward to meeting his Maker and being reunited with the one he had loved for so long. In his mind there was no doubt he would see her soon. She had begun to appear in his dreams, telling him she was waiting for him.

One of his last mornings, Uncle Nick got up from his dreams and found two pieces of cheap cotton twine. He asked his roommate to tie them around his wrists like a bracelet and cut the twine close to the knot. When his friend asked him why, Nick said Julia had told him to. She said wanted something grab onto to help pull him over when his time came.

Three days later, Uncle Nick passed away in his sleep. The twine around his wrists had been pulled so tight it had to be cut away from his flesh. The ends, trimmed close, now protruded conspicuously from the knot.

We are bound together by love. Love unites us because love alone connects us by what is deepest in ourselves.

III. THE MEANING IN LIFE

MEETING GOD

*"The true meaning of love of one's neighbors
is not a command from God which
we are to fulfill, but that through
it and in it we meet God."*
...Martin Buber

Arthur Flemming had the distinction of
serving every President from Coolidge to
Clinton. He was, among other things, a
member of the Hoover Commission,
Secretary of the Department of Health,
Education, and Welfare under Eisenhower,
and head of the Department of Aging under
Nixon and Carter. He also served at different
times as President of five universities.

Before entering public service, Arthur briefly
considered going to divinity school. He
remained devoutly religious all of his life.
For 65 of his 92 years, he attended Foundry
United Methodist Church in Washington,
DC, taught Sunday school during the first

service and sat in the same place - at the end of the fourth pew from the back - for the second service, every Sunday he was in town.

During the week, Arthur had a standing reservation for lunch at Twigs, a restaurant near his office. Arthur held court there, entertaining a revolving cast of regulars and seemingly endless supply of new friends.

At least once a month while he lived, I found myself worked into the rotation. I would receive a call from Arthur's secretary inviting me to join him for lunch, sometimes that same day, sometimes a couple of weeks in advance. I rarely knew Arthur's agenda, but I never turned down an invitation.

We talked about health care reform, one of Arthur's passions. We talked about aging. We talked politics. We talked religion. We talked about life.

On one of these occasions, Arthur began a discourse on applied Christianity. He said the most difficult theological question for him to understand and apply was the notion of loving your neighbor. With a wry smile, he said, "As you have undoubtedly noticed there are a lot of disagreeable people in the world. Some of our neighbors are very difficult to like."

Arthur found the solution to his dilemma in a sermon he heard in England during World War II – a time when the consequences of loving, as well as not loving, our neighbors were abundantly evident. The answer, Arthur said, lies in the difference between *loving* and *liking* and the reason we do one or the other or both.

"You have to remember there is no commandment to *like* our neighbors," Arthur said.

In choosing to love the neighbors we do not like, we separate who we are from what we do. We can love the essence of an individual without liking the choices they have made or the way they live their lives. We can love the sinner without approving of the sin.

THE REVOLUTION OF THE HEART

*"The greatest challenge of the day is how to
bring about a revolution of the heart,
a revolution, which has to start with
each one of us."*
...Dorothy Day

A few years ago, I helped bring a matched
pair of children from the Middle East to Give
Kids the World. Eight-year-old, Maataz
Kishta came from the Palestine. Nine-year-
old Chiam Salinas was from Israel.

Both boys were fighting cancer. Both had
under gone a bone marrow transfer. Both
faced long odds. Both were hoping for a
miracle.

I met them at the airport in New York City.
Almost by design, they seemed to come from
different ends of the plane. Chiam arrived
first, Maataz a few minutes later. They took
positions on opposite sides of me while my

translator helped me greet them and their escorts.

While we waited for the plane to Orlando, they kept as much distance between themselves as possible. Both wanted to know what we had planned for them, but each asked their questions independently. There was no direct communication. They could not avoid being close from time to time, but there was no connection between them.

A week later, after eating together, sharing rides, playing together, and experiencing the wonders of Orlando's theme parks, they left as friends. Somehow along the way, they learned they had more than a disease and a desire to meet Mickey Mouse in common. All they really wanted is what all children fundamentally want - the right to enjoy life and grow up in peace.

"This is the most beautiful thing," Maataz' father, Aatef, told Antonio Mora of NBC News as they were leaving. Chiam's mother, Shula, agreed. "We hope people can learn from this" she said. "I know I have."

If we believe there is one God, if we believe He is the Father of us all, then no child of God can be said to be outside the pale of human kinship and no individual can be considered less human, fundamentally different, or apart. No matter how great and grave the differences between us may appear, below and above all is the eternal fact of brotherhood.

THE COMMON COMMANDMENT

*"Most of the world's great problems
come from love withheld."*
... Roy Burkhardt

In 1991, Edith Lewis went outside to see why
her dog was barking at two in the morning.
She found a teenage boy sleeping in the
bushes by her house.

"He was only 17, but big - like a football
player," she recalled.

When she asked him where he lived and why
he wasn't sleeping at home, she was
surprised to hear him say, "My family
doesn't want me." She was even more
surprised when she called his parents to let
them know the boy was safe.

Instead of responding with the concern she
expected, the boy's father said – "You found

him, you keep him" – and slammed the phone down.

Lewis took the boy in and over the next few months word got around. One kid after another began knocking on her door. Over the years, the ones and twos turned into hundreds, most of them young adults, hardened by the streets, hooked on drugs.

"The general public feels that once they've reached this age – 18, 22, 23, 24 – they'll never get it together and it's a waste of time and money to try to reach them," Lewis said. "They're hungry, they're dirty, they're broke, and they're scared. Most of them have never had an adult in their life they can trust."

Building trust where trust has never been was the biggest challenge. Lewis' secret was her patience and persistence.

"In any other place, the first time the kids cause trouble, they kick them out. The first time they backslide, they are gone," she said. "I just pick them up, dust them off, give them a hug and another chance. After a few months they realize the only reason I do this

is because I really care. Then they start
caring back and I've got them."

*It is no coincidence that every major religion
has at its core some variation of the golden
rule. Most of the world's problems result
from the absence of love, love withheld, or
love denied. The common commandment
asks us to respond by loving each other.*

SYMPATHETIC THREADS

"We cannot live only for ourselves. A thousand fibers connect us with our fellow men; and among those fibers, as sympathetic threads, our actions run as causes, and they come back to us effects."
...Herman Melville

When Bob Macauley was in the sixth grade at Greenwich Country Day School, he remembers a boy who came up from the South. "He was kind of an odd kid," Bob said, "and didn't quite fit in. We had a very tightly knit clique. He looked different and talked different."

Most of the other kids made fun of the Southern boy and gave him a hard time, but Bob befriended him. "He was a long way from home," Bob says. "I used to invite him over to our place on Saturdays and weekends to play." The boy's mother was so grateful she sought out Bob's mother at graduation and thanked her for Bob's kindness. Bob never thought much about it.

Fifty years later, Bob was trying to figure out how to keep his promise to the Pope to help those in need in Poland - the promise that led to the creation of AmeriCares - and looking for whatever assistance he could find. He had volunteers call the leading pharmaceutical companies begging for help. One of them opened a door at the Richardson Vicks Corporation and set up an appointment for Bob two days later.

The community affairs director at the company's headquarters in Wilton listened politely as Bob told his story, but he was noncommittal. As they are about to leave, Bob asked if he could stop by the chairman's office to pay his respects. The director of community affairs said he would see if it was be possible, but he was not optimistic. He said he had been with the company for several years and rarely had a private audience with Mr. Richardson himself. To his surprise, the chairman readily agreed.

When they entered the office, Bob's childhood friend, now Chairman of the Richardson Vicks Corporation, greeted Bob warmly. After they had embraced, Richardson turned to his employee and asked why they were there.

"We are trying to see if we can get some medicines and supplies for Mr. Macauley's foundation," the man explained.

"Not if," the Chairman said. "When."

By the time Bob returned home, the office had already received word there is a freight car full of patent medicines and medical supplies on the way from a Richardson Vicks subsidiary in California. The gifts continued for years.

The nature of the universe is reciprocal.
Things always come back. You help yourself
when you help others.

THE PRISON OF THE SELF

"The first important element of a personal relationship with God is a sense of humility - a sense that letting God into our lives is not the result of our great achievements but of recognizing our limitations."
...Rabbi Harold Kushner

What is the common characteristic of life's failures? What do neurotics, psychotics, criminals, perverts, problem children, and other misfits have in common?

All of life's failures are failures simply because they have not been able to get beyond themselves. They are self-centered and lack social interest.

Most of the evils of mankind would not be possible if the ego did not persuade us that we were somehow different, somehow better, somehow more precious than others. It is the ego that draws the line between "us" and "them" and deludes us into thinking we can go it alone. It is our ego that deludes us into believing that we can be untouched by the problems that plague the rest of humanity or that our problems are of a different magnitude, severity, or degree.

At its worst, the ego can persuade us that our smallest desires are more important than someone else's life, the gratification of our immediate needs more important than another's well-being, or that our view of the way the world should be is more important than the integrity of nations and the lives of thousands.

Conversely, John Ruskin observed, the first test of a truly great man is humility. "I do not mean by humility doubt of his own powers," Ruskin said. "But really great men have a curious feeling that the greatness is not in them but through them. And they see something Divine in every other man."

Ego is the enemy. It keeps us apart. Any activity based on ego and human ambition is a delusion and an obstacle to grace. Ego separates us from those we love and those who love us. It imprisons us in ourselves.

YOUR CHARACTER IS YOUR DESTINY

"Sow an act, and you reap a habit.
Sow a habit, and you reap a character.
Sow a character, and you reap a destiny."
... Charles Read

In the eighties, I ran a small non-profit organization in Washington. It was a start-up operation and my first experience in the non-profit world. We were flying by the seat of our pants, making it up as we went along.

The second person I hired was a young man, Ron Kolanowski, who had wandered in off the streets. Ron was studying to be a priest, but decided to take a break and make sure that this was what he really should do. He was looking for a way to pay the rent while he sorted things out.

On paper, Ron was ill equipped to enter the work force. A head-hunter would have said he had no marketable skills. He had never worked in an office, couldn't type, and new nothing of meetings, membership, budgets, or business.

Still, Ron had a nice way about him and seemed eager to try. I took a chance and put him to work answering the phones, asking him to help out wherever he thought he could.

Ron did whatever we asked and soon owned a piece of every project we had. Before long, he was indispensable. Twenty years later, he had a six-figure income and a role as Vice President of a large company. He walked away from that 10 years ago to return to the seminary and is now an Episcopal priest.

Clearly, Ron learned a great deal while we worked together, he also taught a great deal. One of the things he taught is a particularly valuable lesson: Nothing shapes a person's fate so much as their character. A person with character will do what needs to be done and learn whatever they need to know. Without character, it doesn't matter what you know.

Skills can be learned, but character cannot be taught. Character has to be earned. It is etched into our souls, choice by choice, minute by minute. It is the sum of all we do and the blueprint for all that will follow.

THE MERCHANT OF DEATH

*"I find the great thing in this world is not so
much where we stand, as in what
direction we are moving: To reach
the port of heaven, we must sail
sometimes with the wind and
sometimes against it – but
we must sail, and not drift,
nor lie at anchor."*
... Oliver Wendell Holmes

Alfred Nobel invented dynamite. It was advertised as a "safer" explosive that would bring about a boom in construction, as well as, "prove useful in war." Nobel was so successful, his company soon cornered the market and he became known as the man who revolutionized the art of war.

The fact that this is not how he is now remembered is the result of a curious twist of fate. When Alfred's brother, Ludvig, died in 1888, the newspaper made a mistake and printed Alfred's obituary instead. The headline read: The Merchant of Death is dead.

This sobering gift gave Nobel the perspective he needed to evaluate his life. Out of it came the decision that he wanted to be remembered for something positive and the determination to dedicate his fortune to some good end. As a result, he is generally known today by the awards that bear his name, including, ironically, the Nobel Peace Prize.

We come into the world with empty hands and leave the same way. All we have between coming and going is the use of whatever has been given to us. The rain that falls must nurture the soil it passes through or return to the sea. In the same manner, the gifts we have been given must blossom in others or return unused to their source. The highest and most exalted position, like the grandest house, is only ours to use for a little while.

Our legacy will be determined by the choices we make and the love we give. We are defined by what we do.

PSYCHIC INCOME

*"What we do for ourselves dies with us –
what we do for others remains
and is immortal."*
... Albert Pike

Hugh H. Jones, Jr. has spent a lifetime in the banking business, first with Chemical Bank then with Barnett Banks, where he rose to the position of Chairman and CEO of the Barnett Bank of Jacksonville.

A year after Hugh was named Chairman, the son of a friend underwent unsuccessful heart surgery and died. Looking for a way to help channel his friend's grief and to draw something positive out this negative experience, Hugh began investigating the possibility of establishing a memorial heart program that would benefit other kids in need. When he learned there was no need for such a program in the United States, his thoughts turned to Korea. A veteran of the

Korean War, Hugh knew there were thousands of children in Korea who needed heart surgery.

"The first children we helped arrived on a Friday in March 1985," Hugh remembers. "Two children came in together – a seven-year-old boy and a six year old girl, named Young Joo Yoo. I still have vivid memories of carrying the little girl off the plane, getting the children in the car, and bringing them home."

Hugh did not speak Korean and had no idea how he would communicate with these kids, but he was told not to worry. Sure enough, with a combination of drawing pictures and pointing, Hugh and his wife were able to settle the children in and make them comfortable.

The next evening, Hugh took Yoo to University Hospital to prepare for surgery Monday morning. He stayed with her until she was asleep that night. He returned the next afternoon only to find himself growing increasingly concerned as the surgery approached.

Hugh went home late Sunday night and tried to sleep, but could not. Finally at about 4:00 AM, unable to stand it anymore, he got in his car and went to the hospital to be with the little girl.

"As the nurses came to take her to the operating room, I saw tears in her eyes for the first time," Hugh recalls. "That's when I think a miracle happened."

The girl turned around and lifted her arms up to Hugh as though she thought he would be able to get her through that surgery. By the time he picked her up, there were tears in his eyes, as well, and when he tried to put her down on a mobile stretcher, he found he could not. Instead, he carried her to the operating room, hugging her tightly all the way.

"Those three or four minutes changed my life," Hugh says. "I was working hard and concerned about doing well for the bank, our clients, and myself. I measured progress by the investments I made and the income we received. But that little girl changed me, though to this day she doesn't see how. Now what's important to me is 'psychic income' – the feeling I get when I know I can make a difference in someone's life."

The word "psyche" comes from the ancient Greek. It is the word they used to describe the thing we call the soul. Hugh uses the word in the same sense. When he speaks of "physic income," he means the return on investments that feed the soul.

In the truest sense, we all invest our lives on a daily basis. Our capital is measured in seconds, minutes, hours, days, and years. Each of us is given a finite number to invest for a limited period of time. The fact that the number is not disclosed tells us to invest wisely.

Every choice we make, everything we do is an investment. We can invest in a relationship or in the pursuit of power. We can invest our time in accumulating wealth or in accumulating friends. We can invest in ourselves or in others. We can invest in our own comfort or in our children's future.

Spiritual investments pay the greatest dividends. If you ask Hugh, he will tell you he can't begin to calculate the return on the small investment he made in a little girl's life.

THE GREATEST HAZARD

*"The greatest hazard in life is to risk
nothing. The person who risks
nothing, does nothing, has
nothing, and is nothing."*
...Leo Buscaglia

Brianne Schwantes was born with thirteen
broken bones. All the major bones in her
arms and legs were broken, along with a
number of her ribs. The doctors told
Brianne's parents she would only live a few
hours. The hospital priest was called in to
give her the last rights and her parents cried.
But Brianne wouldn't give up. Somehow,
she made it through the night.

The next day she was diagnosed with a rare
bone disease called Osteogenesis Imperfecta.
The doctors now said they didn't know how
long she would live, but they were certain her
bones were so brittle they would never bear
weight. The doctors told Brianne's parents

she could never have a normal life and live independently. They said that the best thing to do was to put her in an institution and forget about her.

Instead, her parents decided that if Brianne wouldn't give up, they wouldn't give up either. They took her home on a feather pillow, popsicle sticks taped to her limbs as makeshift splints, and went looking for alternatives.

They found a group of physicians who were just starting a research protocol for children with this disease and enrolled her in this program. Brianne was so fragile she could break a bone by sneezing, but they encouraged her to learn to walk and challenged her to grow.

Since then, Brianne has had face surgery, leg surgery, and back surgery. She spent her sixteenth birthday in the emergency room with a neck brace, and has had, in her words, more broken bones than Evil Knievel. But each time, she wouldn't quit. And each time, her fragile body has gotten stronger. She still breaks a bone with the frequency the rest of us get the flu, but nothing can break her spirit

"It's hard to stop listening when people tell you to quit," she says. "It's hard to ignore the world when it seems no one thinks you can succeed; but it gets easier. The first time you believe in yourself enough to accomplish the impossible an inner strength is created that lasts a lifetime."

Strange as it may seem, we often gain more through adversity than good fortune. We learn more from losing than winning. Our appreciation of health is enhanced by illness. Suffering increases our ability to feel joy. Our understanding of the value of life is shaped by our awareness of death. Grief and loss build our capacity for empathy and compassion.

To be blessed we must be willing to step out into the unknown with only faith to face fear. Risk must be taken. If we do not extend ourselves, we simply cannot learn, feel, change, grow, love, or live.

LITTLE SISTER

*"It is possible to give without loving, but it is
impossible to love without giving."*
... Richard Braunstein

At my house, we never knew who would be
joining you for dinner. My mother lost her
mother at an early age. All of her life she
carried vivid memories of being passed from
hand to hand, relative to distant relative,
doing without and never quite feeling like
she belonged. In her house all were
welcome. Everyone belonged.

Food was love. No one ever went away
hungry. After my brother and I grew old
enough to live independently, the chief
beneficiary of my mother's affection was an
Airedale, Cassie, who was so well taken care
of I affectionately nicknamed her "Little
Sister."

Cassie was the runt of the litter, but under Mom's care she grew to be about as wide as she was tall. It was not uncommon to find her cooking an egg or boiling a chicken to "sweeten" the dog's dinner.

At the time it seemed funny. Since then, I have come to understand it as something more – You can't love without giving.

The truth of this observation is borne out daily in the market place. In fact, much of modern commerce is built around this fundamental aspect of our nature. Implicit in many advertisements for goods or services, explicit and inescapable in the buying occasions organized to coincide with celebrations of those we love – Mother's Day, Father's Day, Valentine's Day, and, of course, Christmas – is the knowledge that we can easily be persuaded to demonstrate our affection for someone we love by buying something for them.

The impulse to give to those we love is irresistible. What we call humanitarianism is nothing more than a healthier extension of this basic instinct and a broader, more inclusive love. We give to each other out of love, but the gifts we give pale by comparison to the gift of love itself.

LOVE AND HATE

*"The mentality of an eye for an
eye leaves everyone blind."*
... Martin Luther King

Pat Ireland was shot three times at
Columbine High School, including once in
the head. His dramatic fall from the library
into the arms of waiting SWAT teams
created the most memorable image of that
tragic event. While millions of people
remember that day, hardly anyone knows
much about Pat, what he learned from this
tragic incident, or what he had to say about
the mentality that produced it.

For a year, Pat was silent. He refused to
speak to the media and would not discuss
what happened. Finally at a student rally
organized to mark the first anniversary of this
tragic event, he spoke about what happened
for the first time.

Pat described where he was and what happened and then concluded by saying that day and the days that followed had taught him something about the nature of love and hate, the meaning of courage, and the preciousness of life. Pat asked people to remember those who lost their lives and those who were injured, but to take a moment also to think about their own responsibility.

"The battle against hate begins with simple acts of kindness," he said, "knowing people's names and speaking to everyone. Making a point to just be nice to people."

You can't solve a problem on the same level as it was created. Anger breeds anger. Violence feeds violence. When hate is used to combat hate, hate wins. The only way out of this descending spiral is to rise above and seek higher ground. The only way to drive out of the darkness is to be the light.

<u>LOVE IS LOVE</u>

"Good may be accomplished by small degrees, but it is not thereby rendered small."
... Zeno

A few years ago, I was seated with former President George H. W. Bush at a dinner where he was the guest of honor. The dinner was a benefit for the international relief organization – AmeriCares – founded by his lifelong friend and my mentor, Bob Macauley.

"I have had a chance to meet most of the world's leaders," President Bush said at one point during the evening, "Presidents, Prime Ministers, and a lot of remarkable men and women. I don't impress easily, but I have to say I am in awe of Bob Macauley."

It was a sentiment many shared. AmeriCares has responded to every earthquake, flood, and natural disaster, fed every famine, comforted and cared for the victims of every war in the last quarter of a century. In that time, Macauley and his team have raised and distributed billions of dollars in aid to those in need with an overhead of less than two percent. While few people have the opportunity to save even one life, Bob and AmeriCares can honestly say they have saved millions.

Noteworthy as this is, what made Bob particularly remarkable was his ability to focus on someone's personal problems with the same intensity. Seemingly no global challenge was too large, no personal crisis to small to escape Bob's compassion and concern.

Many people from around the world sought to ease the pain in Bosnia, for example, but only Macauley would think to send a world-class conductor along on one of his relief missions so that the embattled people of that land could celebrate the holidays with music. Only Macauley would think to include millions of pounds of chocolate for the children of Poland along with the emergency supplies sent when that country was under martial law, send a piano or church organ with every shipment sent to rebuild the churches destroyed by hate crimes in the south, or quietly and without fanfare sense and answer the unique personal needs of countless people facing a personal or family crisis. For Bob, it was all one and the same thing.

Differences in degree do not make differences in kind. There are no big lies or small lies, grand larceny or petty theft. A lie is a lie. A thief is a thief. A gift is a gift. Any child is every child. Each life is precious. Every ounce of compassion counts. Love is love.

RESPONSE ABILITY

"To be a man is precisely to be responsible.
It is to feel shame at the sight of what
seems unmerited misery. It is to take
pride in victory won by one's comrades.
It is to feel, when setting one's stone,
that one is contributing to the
building of the world."
...Antoine de Saint-Exupery

The essence of life can be found in what
Viktor Frankl called man's "two-fold
uniqueness" – the uniqueness of the
individual and the moment. In conjunction,
Frankl said, the uniqueness of the moment
and man's response to the moment combine
to give meaning and purpose to our lives.

"Response" is at the root of the word
responsibility. Our ability to respond is the
central fact of our existence. Ten percent of
life has to do with what happens to us. The

other ninety percent is shaped by how we respond.

The constant factor is the need to respond. The variable is each individual's ability to respond in specific ways unique to themselves and their situation in life. We each must act knowing no one else can do what we can do.

Each of us has a specific responsibility particular to our lives and specific to our talents. We must answer for every gift we are given, every talent we possess, every privilege we are granted. We must act in this moment or the possibilities this moment possesses will pass.

Every right implies a responsibility. Every opportunity carries an obligation, every possession a duty.

A DIFFERENT KIND OF HERO

*"Without heroes, we are all plain people and
don't know how far we can go."*
...Bernard Malamud

Easy Eddie was Al Capone's lawyer. At that
time, Capone virtually owned the city of
Chicago. The crime syndicate he had built
on booze had grown to embrace every aspect
of illegal activity from theft to prostitution,
extortion, and murder.

Despite Capone's notoriety and the breadth
of his illegal activities, Easy Eddie succeeded
in keeping him out of jail for a long time.
For this, he was rewarded with more than big
money. He had the run of the town under
Capone's protection. His estate filled an
entire Chicago city block. He lived large and
gave little thought to the atrocities he
supported.

If there was anyone Eddie cared about at all other than himself, it was his son. Eddie saw to it that his young son had the best of everything - clothes, cars, and a good education. Nothing was too good for his son. Price was no object.

And despite his involvement with organized crime, Eddie tried to teach his son right from wrong. He wanted his son to be a better man than he was and that desire led him to make a better man of himself. Eddie realized that all the money in the world couldn't buy the two things he wanted most for his son: a good name and a good example.

With that in mind, he made a difficult decision. He knew the only way he could give his son a good name was to rectify all the wrong he had done. The only way to do that was to go to the authorities and tell the truth about the man they called "Scarface."

With some trepidation, Eddie agreed to testify against the mob even though he knew the cost would be great. But greater than any fear for his own safety was the desire to be a good example to his son. Within a year of his testimony, Eddie's life ended in a blaze of gunfire on a lonely Chicago street. He had given his son the greatest gift he had to offer at the greatest price one could pay.

Butch O'Hare was a different kind of hero. While Easy Eddie's courage was private and personal, Butch's valor earned him recognition as one of the first heroes of World War II.

Butch was a fighter pilot assigned to the aircraft carrier Lexington in the South Pacific. On February 20, 1942, his squadron was sent on a mission. Shortly after he was airborne, he looked at his fuel gauge and realized that someone had forgotten to top off his fuel tank. There was no way he would be able to complete his mission and return to the ship. When he reported in, his flight leader told him to turn around and return to the carrier.

Reluctant to leave his comrades, Butch dropped out of the formation and headed back to the fleet. As he was returning to the mother ship, he saw something that turned his blood cold. A squadron of Japanese bombers was speeding their way towards the American fleet.

With all their fighters gone, the fleet was defenseless. Butch couldn't reach his squadron and bring them back in time to save the fleet. Nor could he warn the fleet of the approaching danger.

So he did the only thing he could do. He decided to take them on by himself.

Laying aside all thoughts of personal safety, Butch dove into the formation of Japanese planes with guns blazing. Butch weaved in and out of the formation, attacking one surprised plane and then another. When his ammunition was spent, he continued the assault by diving into the enemy's planes, trying to clip off a wing or a tail and render them unfit to fly.

Finally, against all odds, he prevailed and the Japanese squadron took off in another direction while Butch and his tattered fighter limped home. The film from the camera mounted on his plane told the tale in graphic detail. Among the things it recorded was the fact that Butch had destroyed five enemy bombers.

As a result, Butch O'Hare became the first Naval Aviator to receive the Congressional Medal of Honor. A year later, he was killed in aerial combat, but his home town refused to allow his memory to pass away with him. O'Hare Airport is named in tribute to the courage of this great man.

While the entire city honored Butch's memory, no one could have been prouder than Easy Eddie would have been if he were still alive. As you may have guessed, Butch O'Hare was Easy Eddie's son.

Your life is your message. What you do speaks louder than anything you can say.

MEANS AND ENDS

*"What you are is the sum of
everything you have done."*
...Buddha

One summer, representatives of American
Airlines walked into Henri Landwirth's
office and offered him a quarter of a million
dollars.   They said they wanted to contribute
to the charity Henri founded – Give Kids the
World.

Henri turned them down.

Give Kids the World is a resort Henri has
built for children facing terminal illness. It is
located in Orlando, Florida, minutes from
Disneyworld. Wish-granting groups from
across the country and many other parts of
the world send thousands of sick children and
their families to this remarkable place every
year. The children eat in a Ginger Bread
House, play in the Castle of Miracles, ride on

their own railroad, and fish in a private pond guaranteed to yield a fish in ten minutes. They stay in their own private villas, receive free tickets and transportation to all the area resorts, and find presents waiting for them on their beds every time they come home.

American Airlines said they had heard all this and were impressed by what Henri and his friends were doing. They said they wanted to be part of the Village, offering to construct a water park where the kids could play. The only condition was that they wanted to put their logo over the entrance.

Henri said, "No."

American Airlines' representatives were surprised and confused. To them it seemed a modest request.

Over 150 companies have contributed to Give Kids the World, Henri explained. All together at that time they contributed more than $20 million a year in services and had helped construct a village worth more than $50 million. None of them advertised their presence or had made any effort to capitalize on their contributions.

"They all understand, " Henri said, "that everything we do here is for the kids. 100%."

With that the American Airlines crew left disappointed. But they returned two weeks later with a check for twice the amount they had originally offered.

They said that when they reported what happened to their Chairman instead of greeting their report with disbelief and anger as they had expected he responded by saying, "It's nice to know there are still some people out there with principles." He told them to double American Airlines' contribution.

The means are the ends. We cannot lie without become a liar. We cannot steal without becoming a thief. We may talk of peace and brotherhood, but until we are, in fact, a brother to everyone, peace will never come and brotherhood is not possible.

BELIEVE AND ACHIEVE

*"The thing always happens that you
really believe in; and the belief
in a thing makes it happen."*
...Frank Lloyd Wright

Claude Pepper knew what he wanted to be
from an early age. When he was ten years
old he carved "Claude Pepper will be a U. S.
Senator" on the back of his bedroom door.
Rather than admonish him for what he did,
his mother reinforced what he said.

After law school, Pepper was elected to the
Florida State Legislature. There, in the halls
of the State Capitol, he met the woman he
would marry. For him, it was love at first
sight.

She was a beauty queen. He would never be
called handsome. For years he carried the
scars of hearing a girl tell a college fraternity
brother trying to fix him up, "I will go out

with any one of your friends except Claude Pepper. He has got to be the homeliest person alive." Pepper was short and fat with a face like a potato.

Still, when Claude saw Mildred, he was undeterred. He walked up to her and introduced himself, saying, "Madame, I am Claude Pepper. Someday I am going to be a United States Senator and I am going to marry you."

Mildred looked the freshman state legislator over carefully and figured there was about as much chance of one as the other. "Oh," she responded with a laugh, "Well, when you are a U. S. Senator, I will marry you."

Claude and Mildred were married the day he was sworn in, one of the youngest Senators in the history of the United States. Later, Pepper became a stalwart of the New Deal, sponsoring the lend-lease legislation that saved Britain and helped turn the tide of the war.

Still later, after a stunning defeat in one of the ugliest Senate campaigns on record,

Pepper, decided to return to Congress. Now 65 and at a point in his life when most people thought he was through, Pepper had just begun. He beat the odds again and served in the House of Representatives until he died at the age of 88.

Pepper said the key to his success was his mother. She believed in him when no one else did and taught him to believe in himself. What we think and believe, we do and become.

IV.   HAPPINESS, JOY, AND SORROW

FINDING HAPPINNESS

"Human beings are not fully happy or
healthy until they serve the purpose
for which God created them."
...Ken Carey

Mother Teresa was a teacher before
beginning her work with the Missionaries of
Charity. While she knew she was doing
good work, she felt called to do something
more. She didn't know what.

"How will I know when I have found my
place?" she asked one of her counselors as
she contemplated the possibilities of a career
change.

He said, "You will know by your happiness."

Most of us have a similar occasion when we
wonder if we are on the right road and
moving in the right direction. Are doing
what we were meant to be doing? Are we

making the best use of our time and talents? Or, are we drifting and taking the path of convenience? It is easy to get discouraged and feel lost.

But discouragement is a reflection of doubt and doubt is a rejection of the gift of the moment. Faith tells us life is a journey. Where we are leads to where we are meant to be.

You know you are on the right path when everything you have done seems to have prepared you for what you are being asked to do. You will know you have arrived when the deepest part of you feels engaged. You will know you are in the right place by the joy it brings.

THE QUICKEST WAY TO IMPROVE
THE WORLD

"Every man, however obscure, however far
removed from the general recognition,
is one of a group of men impressible
for good, and impressible for evil, and
it is in the nature of things that he
cannot really improve himself
without in some degree
improving other men."
... Charles Dickens

John Fling grew up dirt–poor. He was one of
17 children raised on the banks of the
Chattahoochee River. "We weren't
sharecroppers," he said. "We were sharecroppers helpers. There wasn't much that we
ate that we didn't catch out of the water, dig
out of the ground, or shake out of a tree."

When he was old enough to strike out on his
own, John got a job, supervising children
selling newspapers in Columbia, SC. He was

surprised to find many of these children were growing up the same way he had.

"When you have seventy-five to a hundred children with you all day long," John said, "you are going to know where they live and what they need." He began helping out by taking money out of his pocket to buy hungry children something to eat. When I met John 25 years later he was still driving a truck, but his spontaneous acts of compassion had evolved into caring for an extended family that included two hundred children, forty blind people, and over a hundred seniors.

What John did for them was nothing more nor less than most of us do for our own families. He checked on their well being, transported them to medical appointments when necessary, bought them food, kept them company, and responded to their specific needs.

John never asked anyone to share his load. He never passed the hat or held a fundraiser. His approach was simple. He just gave away whatever he had - nearly everything he earned and everything he was given - for forty years. He didn't have a TV, but he gave dozens to others. He didn't own a home, but helped others buy theirs. After a lifetime of work, all he had to his name was enough money to bury whoever died first – himself or his wife.

"It don't matter about who dies second," he said.

Though he never sought publicity, John was known throughout the community. Most everyone you met in Columbia had a positive encounter with him or knew someone he had helped. Even those who had not directly benefited from his goodness seem comforted by the knowledge that such goodness existed in their midst.

People like John make the world a better place simply by being who they are. Their example reminds us we don't need a lot of resources or an elaborate plan to change the world. All we have to do is start where we are, use what we have, and do what we can. The quickest way we can improve the world, is to start with ourselves. The easiest way to teach the truth is to live it.

EVERY DAY CONDUCT

*"The virtue of a man ought to be measured,
not by his extraordinary exertions,
but by his every day conduct."*
...Blaise Pascal

In the summer of 1993, Katie Eller opened a lemonade stand in Tulsa, Oklahoma. She he had just turned nine, but she had a good head for business. Knowing there was a big convention in town, Katie set up her stand across the street, between the hall and the parking lot.

But even she was surprised when cleared $26.27 on her first day. It was so much more than she expected, she was unsure what to do with so much money. After discussing the matter with her family and considering the options, she decided to donate the money to the homeless shelter. Her father took her to the shelter the following day so that she could make her contribution and see where the money was going.

"As entered the doorway," she remembers, "my heart nearly broke when I saw a girl about my own age trying to play under a table in a crowded room."

Katie felt she had to do something about it. From that instinct, Lemon-Aid was born. Katie began recruiting other children, in effect franchising her lemonade stand, as a way to raise money for the homeless. Before she was done, Katie's franchise had grown to a thousand stands, the idle day's experience to a yearly event. Eventually with matching money from local corporations, Katie and her friends were able to raise more than $750,000 and add a wing to the homeless shelter.

When we set out to make a difference, we are tempted to think in terms of heroic acts; but as Katie reminds us that the world is changed from the bottom up more often than from the top down. More often than not, we make a difference not by some single act of momentous consequence but rather by small, sustained acts of caring and compassion.

A LIFE OF LOVE

"The rule of life is to be found within
yourself. Ask yourself constantly,
'What is the right thing to do? Beware
of ever doing that which you are
likely, sooner or later, to
repent of having done."
...Confucius

A few years ago, I visited San Francisco for a
board meeting of the Jane Goodall Institute.
Though I arrived late in the day, I was
determined to get out of the hotel and enjoy
the city.

As I began to walk around, I was surprised
by how much things seemed to have
changed. The area around my hotel felt
uncomfortable. Many of the people on the
street seemed somewhat seedy. The few
shops that were open were the kind of shops
most communities try to close.

Still, my parents were married on O'Farrell Street a few blocks away. I was determined to visit the site and began walking in that direction. As I waited for a light at the first major intersection, I saw a derelict coming toward me. He was dirty and drunk and disheveled. His hair was long and unkempt. His face and clothes were covered with filth.

As he staggered across the street, a gang of rowdy young people entered the intersection from the crossing street. They were loud and obnoxious, clearly out for a night on the town. They took great delight in ridiculing the drunken man as he approached.

Their amusement reached a crescendo when the derelict stopped in the middle of the street, dropped his pants, and began to urinate. He stood there for a moment, wavering and fighting for balance until the booze got the better of him.

He fell and lay there in the intersection, exposed to the world and in obvious confusion. I watched in shock and consternation. The gang of teens ran to his assistance, helping him to his feet, pulling his pants up, and seeing him safely across the street.

It's been five years, but this incident is still fresh in my mind. I don't know which I regret more - that I was not the one to help or that I so badly misjudged those who did.

Each day we meet indifference, ingratitude, disloyalty, dishonesty, greed, ill will, and selfishness. A life of love requires we answer with honesty, integrity, empathy, good will, and selflessness. A life of love asks us to listen with our hearts, act with compassion for all living things and live a life of limited regrets.

THE GREATEST MISTAKE

*"The greatest mistake you can make in life is
to be continually fearing
you will make one."*
...Elbert Hubbard

Richard Nixon was Vice President when
Arthur Flemming served Eisenhower's
cabinet. When Nixon began his first
campaign for President, he asked for and
received Flemming's help.

Near the end of that campaign, Flemming
found himself with Nixon in California. The
combination of Nixon's strong showing there
and a recent statement on Nixon's behalf by
Eisenhower had drawn the election
unpredictably close. Both Nixon and
Flemming knew the campaign was for all
intents and purposes over. As he considered
the possibility that he might lose, Nixon
fixed his attention on polling data showing a

significant shift in his favor after Ike's statement of support.

"Maybe I should have asked Ike to get more involved in the campaign," Nixon said, "but he is the President. It didn't seem appropriate for me to make demands on his time."

Flemming and Nixon parted, knowing the election could go either way.

A week later, Flemming was in the Oval Office meeting with President Eisenhower. The election was by then over and Nixon had lost one of the closest elections in history.

"It's too bad," Eisenhower said. "I really think I could have helped him but it was his campaign. Who was I to intrude?"

It is hard to imagine how different the world would be if Nixon had asked for Eisenhower's help. Would Kennedy have been elected? Would there have been a space program? Would men have walked on the moon? Would there have been a Bay of Pigs or Watergate? Would it have prevented the assassination of President Kennedy, his brother or Martin Luther King? Would there have been a war in Vietnam? How would it have changed the dark decade that followed?

There is no way to know, of course, but it is clear that a simple, personal decision made at that juncture in time by one individual affected everything that followed and all of our lives. Reverse it and much of modern history would unravel.

We are responsible for what we do not do as much as for what we do. If all we do is to try to avoid defeat, we can never claim victory. To be happy, we must be willing to risk heartbreak. To be rich, we must be willing to give up everything we have. To be blessed, we must risk being a fool - giving not getting, reaching out for the hand that may not be there, stepping out into the unknown with only faith to face fear. The cost of living is spending ourselves completely. The greatest regret in life is the knowledge that we may not have done all that we could have done, the sense that we have never fully become ourselves.

THE GREATEST GIFT

*"Giving is the highest expression of potency.
Not he who has much is rich, but he who
gives much."*
...Erich Fromm

I never thought I would be grateful for
Bingo.

After taking care of my mother-in-law, Ann,
at home for years after she had a cerebral
aneurysm, my wife and I finally had to place
her in a nursing home. While it is the only
place she can get the level of care she now
needs, it was difficult for all of us.

My wife took our inability to continue caring
for her mother as something of a personal
failure. For me, the decision resurrected a lot
of painful memories from my days as an
investigator for the U. S. Senate. After that
experience, I swore I would never put a
family member in a nursing home.

Despite my concerns, Ann settled in quickly. While there were indeed some unpleasant aspects to the transition, there were also some pleasant surprises. Chief among these was the joy she took in playing Bingo. Ann plays twice a week and, judging from her accounts, always wins.

I thought the pleasure she took in this pastime was obvious and superficial until Christmas approached. Then on one of our visits, she asked my wife, Angie, to pull a box out from under the bed. Angie held up the box and found a strange assortment of things inside – a book, jewelry, toys, and toiletries.

As we examined the contents of the box, Ann explained she had purchased these things with the points she had won at Bingo. With obvious pleasure, she said they were Christmas gifts she wanted us to wrap for her. After years of being taken care of and continually being on the receiving end, Ann had finally found a way to give. Nothing I have ever experienced spoke more eloquently to the depth of this need than her excitement as she told us about her gifts.

Giving is such fundamental fact of our existence the ability to give can be said to define human development. If you think about it, infancy is a state of total dependence. The transition to adolescence begins when we start to become independent and learn to take care of ourselves. The mark of maturity is when we begin to care for others. The greatest gift is to be able to give.

WRITE IT ON AN ICE CUBE

*"Goodness is the only value that seems in
this world of appearances to have
any claim to be an end in itself.
Virtue is its own reward."*
... William Somerset Maugham

My father's health deteriorated progressively
through the years. The degeneration of his
lungs put an increasing strain on his heart.
Heart problems were followed by kidney
problems, kidney problems by diabetes. It
was as though his bodily systems were
failing, one by one.

Then in the spring of 1988, Dad developed
cataracts and had to go in for surgery on both
eyes. The operation on the first eye went
well, but the second did not. As he waited
for things to heal enough to allow corrective
surgery, he grew increasingly frustrated an
angry. His body had been betraying him for
years. This was the final insult.

During that time, it seemed there was little he could do other than aggravate my mom. Unable to work and uninterested in TV, Dad spent much of his time looking through the mail order catalogs that poured into the house. Dad called them his "wish books." He examined each one that arrived in detail, thumbing through them for hours.

Watching this activity, day after day, and trying to guess why he seemed so preoccupied with something so trivial, frustrated my mother even more. Her frustration was compounded whenever she asked him what he was doing. "I am just looking," Dad always responded defensively. "Can't I look?"

It seemed like a small thing in the midst of some many other things; but it grew to be the source of the greatest friction I ever saw between my parents. Finally, it got so bad my brother and I felt we had to give Mom a break. We agreed he would take her on a mini-vacation, while I stayed with Dad and took care of him.

Almost as soon as we returned from taking them to the airport, Dad pulled out one his wish books. "I have been looking for a ring like this," he said, "and I need your help."

Dad explained that when they were married he could not afford to buy my Mother an engagement ring, but he had promised her that someday he would. Their 45th anniversary was approaching. In anticipation of that event, he had been searching for the perfect ring and a way to make good on his promise.

The ring had to have thirteen stones, Dad said, because they were married on July 13. For the same reason, he wanted the center stone to be a ruby, the birthstone for July, flanked by a smaller ruby and by five diamonds on each side. After months of looking, he said he thought he had finally found what he wanted in one of the catalogues. He asked me to drive him to the store so that he could see it.

We did as Dad wanted, but the ring he had seen advertised was disappointing. The stones were small and of poor quality. There were some other nice rings in the store, but they did match the image he had in his mind and were priced well beyond his means.

Much of the week Mom was gone, we shopped for the ring he wanted without success. My Father was reluctant to give up but the time for her return was rapidly approaching. To put his mind at ease, I assured him that I knew what he wanted and would keep looking until I found it. Dad seemed satisfied with that but he made me promise I would give him the bill.

With that I went to a jeweler in downtown Washington and told him I wanted him to make a ring for me. We picked out the stones and agreed on the price. Then I told him why I wanted the ring and asked for a favor. I said I would pay his price, but I wanted two invoices - one for the full amount, the other made out in the amount my father hoped to pay.

The jeweler was happy to comply and Dad was delighted with ring. He was even more pleased when he saw Mom's reaction to her anniversary ring and her appreciation of the thought and great love that had gone into its purchase.

My father passed away five months later. My mother followed him in eighteen months. Neither one of them ever knew what I had done. While I have done many more things with my life than I would have thought possible, nothing gives me more satisfaction than this. When you do something good, write it on an ice cube.

THE LAST TEMPTATION

"Soul is what connects you to everyone and everything else. It is the sum of all the choices you make. It is where your beliefs and values reside. Soul is the center of our relationship to others."
...Tom Chappell

While I worked at the Senate, I led an investigation of one of the largest nursing home chains in the country. The proprietors of these nursing homes were accused of neglecting their patients to the point where twenty-six people died over the period of six months. Our investigation indicated the cause of death was malnutrition. The owners had simply starved these people to death by minimizing food and withholding nutritional supplements to keep their cost down and maximize profits.

We brought the executives who owned the company that owned the nursing home chain before the Senate to respond to these allegations. At the same time, the State's Attorney General, filed a criminal action indicting the corporation for homicide. As you would expect, the allegation that people were killing those they were supposed to care for caught the press' attention. Media interest was high.

When the hearing convened, the principals of the company foolishly tried to defend themselves by saying all they did was follow common business practices. They regretted the loss of life but justified their actions by saying that like any business they had to make a profit. They suggested any prudent businessman or woman would have done the same thing.

The Committee was outraged. The Chairman, a businessman of some note, was particularly offended. He turned to me and said, "I want to bury these guys. Give me whatever you've got."

While other Committee Members questioned the witnesses, I drafted a series of questions I knew the nursing home owners could not answer without incriminating themselves. When Chairman's turn came, he methodically began going down the list. I watched the members of the Committee seated on either side of him look over the Chairman's shoulder and follow along. I watched them monitoring the press' response. It didn't take long to see where the questions led. Cameras rolled. Members leaned forward in anticipation.

At the last moment, one of the Members sitting near the Chairman asked as a courtesy for a point of clarification. Following Senate protocol, the Chairman graciously agreed, only to see his colleague steal the last question on my list and grab the headline. The Chairman was boxed out. His colleague was the one who made the evening news.

It is the kind of conduct you get accustomed to in Washington. You get used to seeing members posturing and positioning themselves, trying to catch the light. No less common in the world of charity where I now live are the citizens who conditions their gifts on gratitude, expecting the poor unfortunate they have aided to be forever grateful for every scrap of bread they have been handed. While one will claim credit for every favorable shift of the wind, the other would hold you in their debt for their every kindness. Both instincts come from the same self-serving source.

In the words of T. S. Elliott, "The last temptation is the greatest treason - to do the right deed for the wrong reason." Souls are lost in the chasm between doing the right thing and doing the right thing for the right reason.

THE MEASURE OF EXISTENCE

*"Pray that your loneliness may spur you
into finding something to live for,
great enough to die for."*
...Dag Hammarskjold

At various times in my life I have courted
danger. In the military and as a Senate
investigator I came closer to the edge than I
now care to remember. If there was a
dangerous assignment, I sought it. If
someone had to walk in harm's way, I
stepped forward.

I went undercover and carried a wire for the
U. S. Attorney in New York, chased crooks
and corrupt politicians in Chicago, and was
taken for a ride by a wise guy with a gun in a
shoulder holster. I was threatened by high-
priced lawyers, offered bribes, had my home
burglarized, my phone tapped, and my car
nearly torched.

Then I operated in the heat of the moment and in the context of right and wrong, duty and responsibility. There was also a cocky sense of self-confidence often associated with those who are young and feel they are indestructible. Only in the coolness of reflection have I since come to wonder – What is worth giving your life for?

We justly applaud the firefighter who steps into the burning building, police officers who risks their lives to keep our communities safe, or soldiers willing to fight to preserve our way of life. But that answer while accurate seems inadequate. Must we die a hero's death to die for something?

Storming a beach, rescuing a child, or stopping a thief are brave and essential acts. But rarer, less noticed in the world, often more difficult, and perhaps nobler still are the little, nameless, acts of love and kindness that form what William Wordsworth called "the best part of a good man's life."

Ultimately, the only thing we have to give is ourselves. Love requires us to give ourselves away without expecting anything in return.

*But, give we must. If we don't give our lives
for something, we die for nothing. The
measure of our existence is shaped and
fashioned by what we choose to love.*

V. Here and Hereafter

A METAPHOR FOR LIFE

"Yesterday is gone.
Tomorrow has yet to come.
We have only today.
Let us begin."
... Inscription on the front door of
Mother Teresa's house in Calcutta

When Jacques d'Amboise was a child
growing up in Brooklyn, art was the furthest
thing from his mind. Forced to accompany
his sister to dance class, he displayed his
displeasure by mugging, mocking, and
mimicking the girls at every opportunity.

Rather than a reprimand him for disrupting
the class, the girl's instructor responded with
a challenge. "If you are so smart," she said,
"let's see if you can do better." When he
took the bait, she extended the challenge –
"Is that as high as you can jump" – forcing
him to try harder. Almost before he knew it

and against his will, Jacques was caught up in the world of dance.

Two years later, at the age of eight, Jacques was sent to study with Balanchine. He remained the great teacher's favorite pupil and star performer for 40 years.

"Balanchine was wise," Jacques says. "He used music and dance to express his philosophy, which had almost a religious bent. He believed man is meant to be in the service of the arts, the service of mankind, the service of God."

For Jacques, that message translates into an understanding that each individual has within him the possibility of excellence. The purpose of life, as he sees it, is to develop ourselves to the best of our ability and prepare for the opportunity to use our talents.

"Dance is a wonderful metaphor for life," he says. "Every performance is your last performance. It is also your first. You may dance Monday night. But Tuesday you're a different person. And who knows after you dance that night whether you will ever dance again? So each performance becomes the whole world at that moment."

Each instant is its own place – a place we have never been and to which we can never return. What you might have done, you cannot now do. Now presents a whole new set of unique circumstances and choices.

This instant is all that separates what was from what will be. After this moment will come another, but no one can control its content or the opportunities it will present for action. Nor are we guaranteed a role in any moment beyond this. In the next instant, the play may be recast and our role redefined.

THE GIFT OF BEING PRESENT

"That is the problem of life. If we are not here, if we are not in the present moment, fully ourselves, we miss everything."
...Thich Nhat Hanh

Henry Nichols, a hemophiliac, was infected with HIV as a result of a blood transfusion at the age of twelve. At that time, no one could tell what would happen. Some thought he would get AIDS and die right away. Others were more optimistic. They thought he would probably get AIDS and die a few years later.

Back then, living with AIDS for any amount of time was practically impossible. Henry used to joke that he had the life expectancy of a hamster. Seemingly overnight, his sister, Jena, recalls Henry became like Peter Pan – the boy who would never grow up.

Over the years, his family mourned all that Henri would miss. He would never have a chance to get married, to raise a family of his own, to be an adult. While they mourned what he had lost, Henry celebrated what he had left. He made the most of every moment, living life to its fullest.

For most of us, growing up means replacing the things we want to do with things we have to do. We feel we must turn away from the things that delight us, because they are dangerous, impractical or frivolous. No adult, other than John Belushi, for example, would think to cut watermelon with a Samurai Sword. But Henry knew that watermelon sliced with a sword tastes sweeter. Most adults feel the need to plan for the future and set something aside for a rainy day. Henry took life one day at a time and never worried about money. Instead, he invested in life and cultivated friendships.

Henry's approach to life was validated when tragedy compounded tragedy. After battling HIV for years, being in and out of hospitals and finally on the verge of living something close to a normal life, Henry died as a result of an accident.

There is no way to explain the tragic end to such a brave life, but this is certain. Jena was right. While he lived, Henry had magic. His gift was his ability to live in the moment.

The future is now. This is the only moment we have.

THE TEST OF ADVERSITY

*"He knows not his own strength that
has not met adversity."*
...Ben Jonson

A few years before he died, Dr. Norman
Vincent Peale told me about a meeting he
had with the legendary strong man, Jack
Lalane. Though then in his late seventies,
Lalane was still robust and strong,
demonstrating great strength and endurance.
Though only a few years older, Dr. Peale's
body demonstrated the fragility more
commonly associated with advanced age.

"I asked him," Dr. Peale said, "How do you
do it. How does one develop and maintain
such strength?"

"The answer is simple," Lalane said. "You
get strong by challenging your body, by
exercising your muscles against increasingly

heavier weight and testing yourself against increasingly greater resistance."

"That's when it struck me that you get mentally and spiritually strong in just the same way," Dr. Peale said. "We get mentally tough by taking on intellectually difficult questions. We get spiritually strong through suffering and adversity."

Pain and suffering are part of life's refining process. They push us to the limits of what we can do and be. Whatever unwelcome fate befalls us, whatever setback we face or injury we receive, we are challenged, after the first pain and disappointment subside, to see how we can turn it to our benefit.

Adversity introduces us to our true selves. Just as winter reveals the contours of the land, the strength of our character, who we are and what we can be, only emerges when we are tested.

THE LESSON OF THE TREE

*"It is by those who have suffered
that the world is advanced."*
...Leo Tolstoy

When I was a boy of eight or nine, I was walking through the woods in the mountains near home with my Father when we came upon a large tree that had been cut to clear the path. My father pointed to the rings at the cross section where the tree had been cut and asked if I knew their significance.

I gave him the conventional answer telling him I knew the rings of the tree reflected the tree's age. My father said that was right and then he expanded that observation in a way I have never been able to forget.

"If you look closely," he said, "it can also tell you something of the tree's history."

Dad pointed to a narrow band near the tree's center.

"That tells you this was a tough year for this tree. If you count back the rings and determine the date you will probably find that it was a dry year or that the tree faced some other challenge to its growth. Conversely, the broad band tells you the tree had a year of expansive growth."

"But what is most important is the pattern," he said. "Broad bands almost invariably follow narrow bands. That's because in the dry years and difficult periods the tree had to put its roots down deeper in order to survive."

Like the tree, we are all at times challenged and pushed to the limits of our existence. If we are to survive and grow, we must reach deep and draw on the best part of ourselves. Those who cannot find a purpose in their pain are diminished by it. Those who do are strengthened by the process.

THE PROMISE OF PAIN

*"When everything seems to be going against
you, remember that an airplane takes
off against the wind, not with it."*
...Henry Ford

Three years after our walk in the woods, my
Father told me he was dying.

My Grandfather lost his ranch in Colorado
about the time my parents were married. The
combination of bad economic times and the
catastrophic illness of my Aunt Helen proved
to be more than he could handle. Granddad
spent everything he had to help make my
Aunt well, stretching his credit to the limit.
Finally, one last bad season tipped the
balance. The ranch was liquidated, the
livestock sold. My father lost what would
have been his inheritance, had to look for
work, and wound up in the coal mines of
Southeastern Utah.

On that fatal day, my Father had gone to the doctor for the annual physical required by the company. He went in expecting nothing and feeling fine only to find out he had Black Lung and that his days were numbered. At best, they said, he had five years to live.

I remember it vividly even now. I remember the pain and irony I felt as the entire landscape of my father's life suddenly came into view: a man raised outdoors with a love of nature and open spaces, forced to leave the light and go underground; the need to support his parents and then feed his family postponing then eliminating any hope he had of getting an education; a man who had never smoked so much as one cigarette in his life acquiring a disease most commonly associated with heavy smoking.

The dreams of the father are often revealed in the son. At that moment, my Father's hopes and dreams became mine to carry. After he told me what the doctors had said, he extracted a promise.

"You know how much I want you to get an education," he said, "It looks like I'm not going to be here to help you. I want you to promise me that somehow you will find a way to do what I couldn't do and finish school."

There was no choice, of course. And so I made the promise he requested not knowing how I would be able to do what no one in my family had ever done before. Through the grace of God and with a lot of help, I was able to keep my promise, get a college education and go on to law school. With that achievement came many benefits, but none greater than what I learned about myself.

We become fuller and more ourselves every time we do the thing we think we cannot do. We gain courage with every fear we face, strength with every challenge we meet, and confidence with every obstacle we overcome. There is a promise in every pain.

THE SOUL SET ON FIRE

*"The most powerful weapon on earth
is the soul set on fire."*
...B. C. Forbes

The last of the human freedoms, and therefore the greatest, Viktor Frankl taught, is attitude.

"In the concentrations camps," he said, "the Nazi's took everything away from us. We were under their complete control. They could do whatever they wanted to us. But the one thing they could never control was how we chose to respond to whatever they did to us."

As an example of the transforming power of personal choice, Viktor told me the story of another survivor of the concentration camps who was known for wearing a bracelet made of baby teeth mounted in gold.

"My first reaction when I saw it was that it was beautiful," Viktor said, "and I told her so."

"Yes," the woman responded, "this tooth belonged to Miriam, that one to Esther, and this one to Samuel...", mentioning the names of her nine children before adding they had all been taken to the gas chamber.

Now shocked and surprised, Dr. Frankl said he couldn't help asking, "How can you live with such a bracelet?"

Quietly, the woman replied, "How could I live without it? I am now in charge of the largest orphanage in Israel."

While our talents allow us to express our uniqueness, suffering and pain demonstrate our commonalty. One defines the need for the other and provides a context for action. The end for which the means were meant is to create community. Pain and suffering break down the barriers between us, end our isolation, and put us in touch with the whole human condition.

Those who have suffered deeply speak a language everyone can understand. The deeper our sorrow, the more capacity is created for joy. The more our lives are etched by suffering, the more compassionate we can become.

D = S - M

"Despair is suffering without meaning."
...Viktor Frankl

After my father died, my mother became my greatest concern. My parents had known each other most of their lives. Taking care of him and raising her family had been the focus of her life. I knew she missed him terribly.

I could always talk with my Mother about anything so when I saw an opportunity I shared my concern. To my surprise, she said that it was difficult but it was also a gift in a way. Dad had been sick much of his life, she explained, and had already suffered so much. "Can you imagine how difficult it would have been for him if I had gone first?"

With that I began to see her suffering in a new light. Far from an act of desperation, it was, in fact, an act of faith and fidelity. For years we had shared a wish we could do something to ease Dad's pain with little success. Now, she was saying, at least I can spare him this.

When I told Viktor Frankl my mother's story, he took out one the black Flair pens he liked and wrote an equation: $D = S - M$. "Despair is suffering without meaning," he explained.

Each of us is challenged to find the meaning in our suffering and use it to give purpose to our lives. The greater the pain, the larger the obstacle, the stiffer the resistance, and more hopeless the situation, the greater the reward and more miraculous the outcome can be.

THE CHOICE

*"I thank God for my handicaps, for through
them, I have found myself,
my work, and my God."
...Helen Keller*

My Aunt Helen was paralyzed when she was
twelve. I never received a satisfactory
answer as to the cause. I only know that
whatever came on her came suddenly and
that my grandfather spent everything he had
trying to make her well. Finally, in
desperation he took her to the Mayo Clinic
where they tried a risky experimental
surgery. In the process, her spinal chord was
damaged, ending any hope she would ever
walk upright again.

As a result of the disease or the treatment or
perhaps both, Aunt Helen was paralyzed for
life in a sitting position. She was able to
move her legs but she was never able to
straighten her back or extend her body.

Since she refused a wheelchair, she moved facing the ground, bent over and supporting herself by holding on to someone's arm or leaning on furniture.

Aunt Helen attracted a great deal of attention wherever she went, but not for the reason you might think. People were drawn to her because she was about the most joyful person they had ever met. Her internal joyfulness stood in stark contrast to her external condition.

There was no accident in that. Aunt Helen felt God had made her the way she was for a purpose and in her mind, that purpose was to be an example to others. "If I can be happy," she would say, "What's your excuse?"

Love sustains all, transcends all, makes all things possible, and all conditions of life tolerable. There is no cross that love can't bear.

A TALENT FOR LIFE

*"What I do today is important because I am
exchanging a day of my life for it."*
...Hugh Mulligan

Rob Torres is a professional entertainer. He
has worked for Disney both here and in
Japan, traveled with The Big Apple Circus,
and toured Europe even while still on the
shady side of thirty.

He reminds me a bit of Jim Carrey. He has a
lot of the same mannerism and energy, and
the same wacky sense of humor. Rob is a
very talented young man; but what makes
him most remarkable is not his talent as a
performer, but his talent for life.

Rob is the only person I know, who stops
every day, wherever he is to watch the
sunset. Many people talk about stopping to
smell the roses. Rob does.

When he passes through in the winter, he is always wearing a new coat. Every time he visits he disappears for a while and comes back without it. Though he never dwells on it, you can tell he has found someone who needs it more than he does.

When Rob was eighteen, he stopped by on his way to an audition for his first big job. He parked his car near where I then lived in Washington and spent the night. In the morning we found the entire contents of his car scattered in the streets. The police said some kids had broken in searching for something of value. In the process, they destroyed everything Rob had, including the props he needed to support his act.

I was devastated. Rob laughed it off. He stopped at a thrift store on the way of town, bought some new props, and then invented an act to go with them as he drove to his audition.

If you wonder why Rob lives so fully and completely, he will tell you the reason is that as a boy he fell into a neighbor's swimming pool and nearly drowned. His mother found him literally at the last moment. His heart had already stopped beating. Another second or two would have pushed him beyond the hope of recovery. When you live with a realization like that, Rob says, only a fool would not be grateful. Not many men get a second chance at life.

Most of us spend a lot of time wondering when our lives will come to an end. We think of death as an enemy and dread the day of our demise. Yet, life is defined by death. It is the inevitability of death that focuses our energies and gives meaning to life.

HEAVEN ON EARTH

*"If everyone did an act of daily kindness to
his neighbor and refused to do any
unkindness, half the sorrow of
the world would be lifted
and disappear."*
...John B. Watson

"The very fact that God has placed a certain
soul in your way is a sign that God wants you
to do something for them," Mother Teresa
said. Her order, The Missionaries of Charity,
was founded on this truth. I am one of those
who can testify to its power.

I had the privilege of meeting Mother Teresa
in 1985 when she was in Washington for the
opening of one of her homes. My brother
and I went to meet her with some vague
notion of helping her raise money for her
work. To my surprise she didn't seem at all
interested in what we could do for her. She

dismissed our offer out of hand, saying she preferred to let Providence provide.

Instead, Mother Teresa chose to focus the conversation on what we were doing. In a few minutes she drew out of me things I had thought but could never before articulate. I left her with the sense that I could and should do something more than I was doing and the embryonic thought of what that might be.

There can only be one Mother Teresa, but her truth speaks to us all. God has given each of us the capacity to achieve some end necessary to others. Each of us has the power to increase the sum of the world's happiness.

Everyone makes a difference. The humblest among us can, by shear act of will, help create heaven on earth.

WHERE IS HELL?

"Human nature is such that without other humans we cannot survive."
...Tenzin Gyatzo, 14th Dali Lama of Tibet

Where is hell? What does it look like? Is it fiery and hot or dark and cold? Does it exist at all outside of our minds?

I visited hell in 1992. It was in an AIDS ward in an LA hospital. There I met a young black woman, clinging to life but already in purgatory. She was in a gray place - neither dark or light, hot or cold - caught in transition between the best and worst of her life. She was tormented by the demons of her past, years on the street, and a dependence on drugs, but sustained by love.

The staff attending her was literally counting the days. Most were surprised she had held on so long. What kept her alive, I was told, was her fierce determination to make sure her six-year old daughter was taken care of after she was gone.

The word "hell" comes from the old English. Literally, it means "to separate" or "to build a wall around." To be "helled" was to be shut off.

All those who love can relate to the torment this woman felt on being separated from the one she loved most deeply. Hell is there and everywhere we set ourselves apart.

"Diabolic" comes from a word meaning "to divide." Diabolic forces separate us from each other and God. In our lives they find expression in ego, anger, pride, radical religions, nationalism, racism, envy, ignorance, and greed. These are the forces of darkness. They divide and conquer. By contrast, "heaven" means "harmony." If demonic forces divide, love unites.

The Kingdom of God will arrive on earth when we are able to get beyond the superficial elements that divide us. The only thing that separates us from God and each other is the belief that we are separate.

WHEN IS JUDGMENT DAY?

"I shall tell you a great secret. Do not wait for the last judgment.
It takes place every day."
...Albert Camus

As a boy, I worked at a family grocery store in the small town where I grew up. One summer day as I was taking out the garbage, I was startled by a furtive figure fleeing from the back of the store. It was a strange looking little man dressed all in black. He was wearing the kind of long overcoat cowboys call a duster even though we were in the middle of summer and temperatures approached ninety. He was stuffing something inside a green, canvas bag as he fled.

My first thought was that he was a thief but I could not imagine what he found worth stealing on the loading dock of our store. Later, I learned he was a miser known as

"Little George." Though he received some assistance from public aid, Little George preferred living off what other people threw away, foraging through garbage cans for food, scrounging the neighborhood for tin cans and bottles and other things of potential value.

Along with a wife I never met, Little George lived in a dilapidated house on the south side of town. The windows were boarded up, letting little light in and even less out. Rumor had it, his wife was blind and completely dependent on him. It was said he fed her what he found in other people's garbage cans.

Little George was such a vivid character, I found myself thinking about him off and on long after I had left home. I couldn't help wondering what became of him. Finally years later, one of my relatives filled in the blanks.

She said that shortly after Little George's wife passed away, he was found wandering the streets. He was hospitalized, dazed and confused, suffering from malnutrition and dehydration. The attendants bathed and shaved him and gave him some fluids intravenously. Out of the kindness of their hearts, the staff took up a collection for him and got him some new clothes.

Rather than express gratitude when he came around, Little George accused the hospital of holding him against his will and stealing his things. He insisted on being released and demanded his clothes be returned immediately.

When he was told he could not be released without the attending physician's authorization, Little George became agitated. Bad became worse when he learned the staff had decided his old clothes were so worn and filthy they had to be destroyed. He grew violent he had to be restrained.

Finally, it was too much for him. Little George collapsed, moaning to himself. The reason for his distress soon became clear. He had stuffed the lining of the long black coat he had always worn with the money he had hoarded through the years.

On earth, there are only consequences and actions. Every day is Judgment Day. Every virtue is rewarded. Every crime is punished. Every wrong is redressed in silence and in certainty. The consequences of our indifference, mean-spiritedness, and destructive behavior rebound to our detriment as surely as every act of kindness and compassion returns to our benefit. We are punished not so much for our sins as by them.

THE DANCE

*"I think it not improbable that man, like the
grub that prepares a chamber for
the winged thing it never has seen
but is to be – may have cosmic
destinies he does not understand."*
...Oliver Wendell Holmes, Jr.

My Father and Mother died within months of
each other. After my Mother died, my
brother and I took our parents' ashes down to
the beach. The Outer Banks of North
Carolina had become their favorite place.
Whenever they could, they escaped to the
house we had built there. It was the place we
knew they always wanted to be.

And so, on a stark clear morning in April my
brother and I found ourselves on the beach in
front of their house, each holding a bag
seemingly too small to contain what
remained of our parents. We had generally
agreed we would sprinkle half of what we

carried on the beach and then exchange bags, but neither one of us knew how to begin.

My brother held our Father's ashes. I held Mom's. With some trepidation, I opened the bag I had and gingerly started sprinkling her ashes on the beach, reluctant to let go of what for so long had been the most important person in my life. As if in response to my thoughts, a sudden gust of wind came from nowhere, caught the ashes I had thrown and blew them back directly at me, covering me from head to toe.

I stood paralyzed as a mixture of emotions washed over me. There are no words to describe all I felt, but I have to confess my first instinct was one of horror. I wanted to brush the ashes off my clothes, I wanted to run, but could not.

The wind disappeared as quickly as it had come. In the calm, I was finally, I was able to look for my brother and saw that he was continuing what he was doing, either unaware or unaffected by what had happened.

As I stood there, the enormity of the moment struck me as suddenly as the gust of wind. My fears dissolved. I knew my mother would always be with me.

Life is seamless, stretching forward into the future and back beyond the boundaries of time. The same atoms that dance in us dance in everything in the universe. When we die, nothing ends. The best part of our selves just learns a new dance.

There is no beginning. There is no end. As long as we are loved, we are immortal.

LIGHT FOLLOWS DARKNESS

*"You have been told that life is darkness and
in your weariness you echo what was
said by the weary. And I say that life is
indeed darkness, save when there is urge,
and all urge is blind save when there is
knowledge. And all knowledge is vain save
when there is work, and all work is empty
save when there is love; and when
you work with love, you bind
yourself to yourself, and
to one another, and to God."*
... Kahil Gibran

On a clear day in September 2001, the forces of darkness conspired to break a thousand hearts and change the world.

Minutes after a plane hit the second tower, Tim Love, a member of The Heart of America Foundation's Advisory Board, called and said we have to do something. Within days we launched an effort designed to aid the families of those most directly affected by this tragedy, setting up the Heart of America's Family Relief Fund.

Millions of people and hundreds of agencies responded in much the same way. Over 200 organizations created funds designed to help those in need. Over sixty percent of the people in America contributed to this effort.

The ebb and flow of darkness and light can be seen in this challenge and response. At every moment, we have a choice.

Do we want to add more love to the world or less?

Do we want add more honesty to the world or less?

Do we want to add more forgiveness to the world or less?

Do we want to add more gratitude to the world or less?

Do we want to add more justice to the world or less?

Do we want to be part of the community of hope or give in to fear and despair?

Like everything else that lives, we grow toward the light. The more we love, the closer we come to God.

GOD WAITS

"For each of us, there is only one thing necessary – to fulfill our own destiny according to God's will and be what God wants us to be."
...Thomas Merton

As this is written, my son is three years old. Those who have children will recognize the wonder of this age. Daily, my son seems to grow and develop before my eyes. Each day brings a new discovery. With each day he learns something new. With each day he becomes more aware and does something he could not do the day before.

The delight I take in him is sweetened by the fact that I came to fatherhood late in life. Now as I watch him grow one of my greatest hopes is that I live long enough to see him become who he can be. At the moment, all I see is promise and possibilities. How will he respond to the gifts he has been given?

In much the same way, the Father of us all is wondering and waiting. What will we do with the gifts we have been given? How will we exercise our talents and abilities? To what use and purpose will we commit our lives?

We are not God, but we are of God. To each of us is given the opportunity to shape and define the quality of the world we live in. To each of us is given free will and the opportunity to make things better or worse. To each of us is given power equal to our dreams and energy equal to our aspirations.

The legacy of the father is the deeds of his children. God is waiting.

GOD WEEPS

"The course of human history is determined not by what happens in the skies, but what takes place in our hearts."
...Sir Arthur Keith

There is a piece in each of us that is God's piece. In some, that piece is nurtured and grows until it encompasses the sum of their being. In others, it diminishes with neglect and denial until it nearly disappears.

God's piece is the part we call our humanity. This is the piece that responds with care and compassion. This is the part that reaches out with kindness and concern. This is the part that weeps each time we choose comfort over concern.

God weeps when we see and do not act, hear and do not respond.

God weeps when we turn our backs, close our doors, and live apart.

God weeps at the way we offend nature.

God weeps at man's inhumanity to man.

God weeps at our preoccupation with the material means to an end without considering the spiritual end for which the means were designed.

God weeps when we are unfaithful to Him and when we lose faith in ourselves.

God weeps at our arrogance, aggression, and indifference.

God weeps at our carelessness and apathy.

God weeps at every self-centered act that focuses on our needy grasping selves and every act of ego that takes us further away from Him.

IN GOD'S EYE

*"We must judge a man's merits not by his
great qualities, but by the use
he makes off them."*
...Francois de La Rochefoucauld

The value of our lives is measured not by our occasional departures but by our every day conduct, not by our extraordinary contributions but by the weighted average of our lifetime's activities and actions. In the words of Thomas Jefferson, "It is from our lives and not our words that our religion must be read."

In God's eye, we are judged not by the qualities we were given, but by the use we make of what we were given.

In God's eye, the midnight march of a solitary mother holding a sick child has more merit than the march of armies with kingdoms at stake. Kingdoms come and kingdoms go, but love is eternal.

In God's eye, the splendor of titles, the pursuit of power, and the accumulation of material things are all exercises in futility and denial. There is more value in your smallest act of kindness than all these vanities.

In God's eye, the man who dies rich dies disgraced. It is a harsh truth, but all good things in this world have no good beyond their use. We show our wealth more by using it than in having it.

In God's eye, no one is truly great until they understand their life does not belong to themselves alone but to all mankind. What God has given us God has given us for a purpose beyond ourselves.

In God's eye, what makes us great is the degree to which we reflect His being, the degree to which we radiate His light, and the degree to which we love others as He loves us. *What we do with what we have is more important than what we have.*

V. SUMMARY AND CONCLUSIONS

THE PARADOXES OF LIFE

*"Human existence – at least as long as it has
not been neurotically distorted – is
always directed to something, or
someone other than itself be it a
meaning to fulfill or another
human being to love."*
... Viktor Frankl

A string of related paradoxes springs from
the design of the universe. Like the vertebras
that support our flesh, these principles
support the fabric of our lives:

Life is about giving not getting.

You get what you give.

You cannot find happiness until you forget to
seek it.

You cannot serve another without at the same
time serving yourself.

You cannot love without being loved.

To be forgiven, you must forgive.

To get the most out of life, you must consciously strive to put the most into it.

The most selfish thing you can do is to be unselfish.

You find your life by giving it away.

God will not be outdone. We are always paid "in kind." God's attitude toward us is always regulated by our attitude toward others. Seeds of reciprocity are planted with our every act. Generosity, compassion, understanding, and love or suspicion, envy, anger, and distrust always return to us in equal kind and measure.

THE LAWS OF THE HEART

*"Love is not one of the attributes of God but
the sum of them all."*
...James Gibbons

Love is the essence of the soul and these are
the laws of the heart:

Nothing of value can be accomplished
without love.

You cannot love without giving.

The only way to have love is to give it.

To be real, love must be unconditional.

You cannot truly understand anything unless
you love it.

We are shaped and fashioned by what we
love.

Love multiplies happiness and divides sorrow.

Love is the only thing you cannot get enough of and the only thing you can never give enough of.

No matter what the problem is the answer will be always be found when you surround it with love.

It is by loving and giving that we find meaning and purpose for our lives.

Love is all we have. Love is all we need.

God loves the world through us.

What makes us different is not our ability to think, but our ability to love. The heart is the image of God.

77 GUIDING PRINCIPLES
FOR A MORE MEANINGFUL LIFE

1. We Are Here To Serve One Another
    (Confucius)
2. Each Of Us Holds The Answer To
Someone's Prayers
    (Albert Einstein)
3. The Most Selfish Thing We Can Do Is To
Be Selfless
    (W. Beran Wolfe)
4. You Get What You Give
    (Henry Ward Beecher)
5. The Greatest Defeat We Can Suffer Is the
Distance Between What We Are And What
We Can Be
    (Rollo May)
6. It's Love That Acts
    (Buckminister Fuller)
7. To Be Real, Love Must Be Unconditional
    (Elisabeth Kubler-Ross)
8. It Only Takes a Single Ray of Light to
Penetrate the Dark
    (Erasmus)

9. God Is At The Heart Of Everything
    (Robert Frost)
10. Prayer Is The Language Of The Heart
    (St.Teresa)
11. Compassion Is Man's Highest Attribute
    (Sir Thomas Browne)
12. The Only Things Of Real Value In Life
Are The Things That Cannot Be Replaced
    (Barbara Bush)
13. The Things Of Greatest Value In Life
Are The Things We Can Share Without
Diminishing By Sharing
    (James Keller)
14. The More We Are Given, The More
There Is That Is Required of Us
    (John Randolph)
15. Love Is The Essence Of The Soul
    (James Gibbons)
16. There Are No Permanent Solutions
    (Anonymous)
17. The Material Is Immaterial
    (Pierre Teilhard De Chardin)
18. Forgive And Forget
    (Buddha)
19. Life Questions Man
    (Hillel)
20. Nothing Of Value Can Be Accomplished
Without Faith

(Mary McLeod Bethune)
21. Man Cannot Live Without Hope
(Antoine de Saint-Exupery)
22. God Rarely Gives A Truly Big Idea To Only One Person
(Rollo May)
23. There Is No Distance Between Souls
(St. Francis of Sales)
24. All Life Is Sacred
(Chief Seattle)
25. God Speaks With Silence
(Albert Schweitzer)
26. God Has No Religion
(Ghandi)
27. When We Are Engaged In Helping Others, We Are Not So Much Conferring Favors As Canceling Debts
(Ralph Waldo Emerson)
28. The World Was Created For The Purpose Of Giving
(James Gibbons)
29. Nothing Of Value Can Be Accomplished Alone
(Martin Luther King)
30. The Greatest Good We Can Do Is Not To Share Our Wealth With Others But To Reveal To Them Their Own
(e.e. cummings)

31. No Gift Is Truly Ours Until God Has
Blessed Someone Else With It Through Us
(Andrew Harvey)
32. Every Person In Our Lives Is There For
A Purpose
(Richard D. Bach)
33. We Need Each Other
(Erich Fromm)
34. What Happens To One Is Often For The
Benefit Of Another
(Luciano de Crescenzo)
35. Love Connects Us By The Deepest Part
Of Ourselves
(George MacDonald)
36. There Is No Commandment To Like
Your Neighbors
(Martin Buber)
37. No Matter How Great The Differences
May Seem Between Us, Below and Above
All Is The Eternal Fact Of Brotherhood
(Dorothy Day)
38. Most Of The World's Problems Result
From The Absence Of Love, Love Withheld,
Or Love Denied
(Roy Burkhardt)
39. You Help Yourself When You Help
Others
(Herman Melville)

40. Ego Is The Enemy
    (Rabbi Harold Kushner)
41. Your Character Is Your Destiny
    (Charles Read)
42. You Are What You Do
    (Oliver Wendell Holmes)
43. Spiritual Investments Pay The Greatest
Dividends
    (Albert Pike)
44. Risks Must Be Taken
    (Leo Buscaglia)
45. You Can't Love Without Giving
    (Richard Braunstein)
46. You Can't Solve a Problem On The
Same Level As It Was Created
    (Martin Luther King)
47. Love Is Love
    (Zeno)
48. Every Right Implies A Responsibility
    (Antoine de Saint-Exupery)
49. Your Life Is Your Message
    (Bernard Malamud)
50. The Means Are The Ends
    (Buddha)
51. What We Think and Believe, We Do and
Become
    (Frank Lloyd Wright)

52. You Will Know the Right Place By The Joy It Brings
     (Ken Carey)
53. The Quickest Way To Improve The World Is To Start With Yourself
     (Charles Dickens)
54. More Often Than Not, We Make A Difference Not By Some Single Act Of Momentous Consequence But Rather By Small, Sustained Acts Of Caring And Compassion
     (Blasie Pascal)
55. Live A Life of Limited Regrets
     (Confucius)
56. The Greatest Regret In Life Is The Sense We Have Never Fully Become Ourselves
     (Elbert Hubbard)
57. The Greatest Gift Is To Be Able To Give
     (Erich Fromm)
58. When You Do Something Good, Write It On An Ice Cube
     (William Somerset Maugham)
59. Souls Are Lost in the Distance Between Doing the Right Thing and Doing the Right Thing for the Right Reason
     (Tom Chappell)
60. Our Existence Is Shaped By What We Choose To Love

(Dag Hammarskjold)
61. All We Have Is Today
(Mother Teresa)
62. The Future Is Now
(Thich Nhat Hanh)
63. Adversity Introduces Us To Our True Selves
(Ben Jonson)
64. If We Are To Grow And Thrive, We Must Draw On The Best Part Of Ourselves
(Leo Tolstoy)
65. There Is A Promise In Every Pain
(Henry Ford)
66. The More Our Lives Are Etched By Suffering The More Compassionate We Can Become
(B.C. Forbes)
67. Despair Is Suffering Without Meaning
(Viktor Frankl)
68. There Is No Cross Love Can't Bear
(Helen Keller)
69. Life is Defined by Death
(Hugh Mulligan)
70. Everyone Makes a Difference
(John B. Watson)
71. The Only Thing That Separates Us From God Is The Belief That We Are Separate
(Tenzin Gyatzo, 14th Dali Lama)

72. We Are Punished Not So Much For Our Sins As By Them
   (Albert Camus)
73. When We Die Nothing Ends
   (Oliver Wendell Holmes, Jr.)
74. We Grow Toward The Light
   (Kahil Gibran)
75. God Waits
   (Thomas Merton)
76. God Weeps
   (Sir Arthur Keith)
77. What We Do With What We Have Is More Important Than What We Have
   (Francois de La Rochefoucauld)

OTHER BOOKS BY BILL HALAMANDARIS

Be The Light
Love and Hate
His Name Is Today
Quotations from the Heart
The Heart of America: Ten Core Values that
Make Our Country Great
The Hill
The Care Gaps

Made in the USA
Charleston, SC
04 January 2012